Contents

Section Four: Food, shops and shopping 70

Section Five: The world of nature 81

Section Six: Adjectives, verbs and prepositions 96

Check 2 (based on Sections 4–6) 121

Introduction

Target Vocabulary 1 is intended for elementary/pre-intermediate students and presents and practises approximately 1,100 key words. To facilitate learning, these have been arranged into areas of vocabulary. Altogether there are six main sections and each section has between 10 and 12 areas of vocabulary, closely linked to the main theme.

At the end of Section Three and Section Six there are mini tests called Check 1 and Check 2. These checks are for reinforcement and test the items in Sections 1–3 and 4–6 in a varied and interesting way.

Finally, to aid self-study, there is an answer key at the back of the book, plus a list of the key words used and the section(s) in which they appear.

In writing this book I have consulted a number of different dictionaries. The following can be warmly recommended:

Longman Dictionary of Contemporary English – new edition (Longman)
Collins Cobuild Essential English Dictionary (Collins)
Oxford Advanced Learners Dictionary (Oxford University Press)
The Penguin Wordmaster Dictionary, Manser and Turton (Penguin)
BBC English Dictionary (BBC English/HarperCollins)

Section One: People

Personal details
Put the following words in the correct places 1–10 in the form below.

Age	Married or single
Children	Nationality
Christian name	Street
Country	Surname
Job	Town/Village

1_____ Smith

2_____ William

3_____ thirty-six

Address 4_____ 64 Highland Road

          5_____ Bournemouth

          6_____ England

7_____ Canadian

8_____ married

9_____ 1 boy, 2 girls

10_____ taxi driver

The family

Here is the family tree of the Moon family.

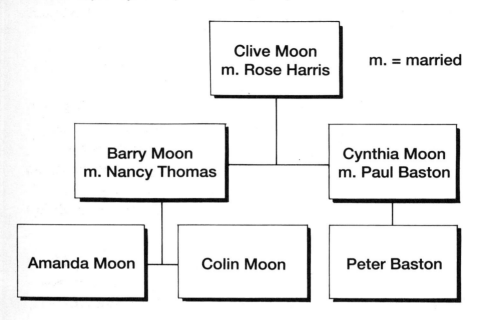

Study the family tree, then write the missing words in the passage below. Choose from the following:

aunt	granddaughter	nephew
brother	grandfather	niece
children	grandmother	parents
cousin	grandparents	sister
daughter	grandson	son
father	husband	uncle
grandchildren	mother	wife

Clive Moon married Rose Harris in September 1940. They had two (1)_____ – a boy called Barry and a girl called Cynthia. Barry met his (2)_____, Nancy Thomas, at university and they got married five years later. In 1974, their

(3)_____, Amanda, was born. The same year, Barry's
(4)_____, Cynthia, met her (5)_____, Paul
Baston. She asked her (6)_____, Barry, to be best-man
at their wedding.

Not long after the wedding, Nancy and Barry had a
(7)_____. They called him Colin. Barry's
(8)_____, Rose and Clive, were thrilled. Now they had
two (9)_____. Soon they would have three. In 1982,
their second (10)_____, Peter, was born. This also
meant that Barry was now an (11)_____ and Nancy an
(12)_____. Both were very fond of their new
(13)_____, Peter, and pleased that their own children
now had a (14)_____.

In 1992, on Amanda's 18th birthday, the Moon family held a
big birthday party. Amanda's (15)_____, Nancy, gave
her a computer – something she had wanted for a long time –
and her (16)_____, Barry, paid for twelve driving
lessons. Cynthia and Paul gave their (17)_____ a
personal CD-player, while her (18)_____, Clive and
Rose, gave her some money. As her (19)_____, Clive,
said, 'Well, it's difficult to buy things for young people, isn't it?'

Amanda's (20)_____, Rose, agreed. 'Our
(21)_____'s taste in clothes is not the same as ours. So
it's much better to let her choose for herself, really.'

Parts of the body: The face

Look at the drawing below and write the correct numbers 1–16 next to the following words.

cheek	eyebrow	jaw	nose
chin	eyelashes	lip	teeth
ear	forehead	mouth	throat
eye	hair	neck	tongue

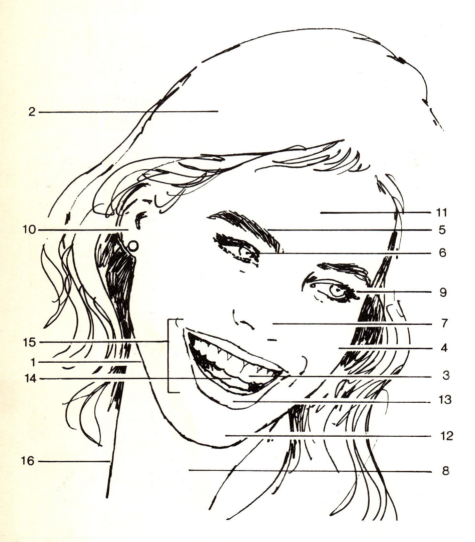

Parts of the body: The body

Look at the drawing below and write the correct numbers 1–20 next to the following words.

ankle	elbow	heel	thigh
arm	finger	knee	thumb
back	foot	leg	toe
bottom	hand	shoulder	waist
chest	head	stomach	wrist

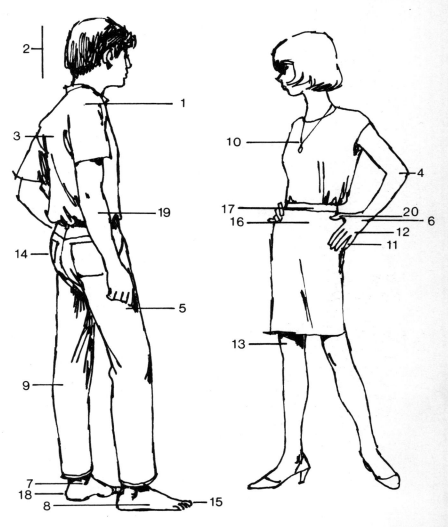

Verbs to describe daily routines

Read about Linda Taylor's typical day below and supply the missing verbs 1–30. Choose from the following:

brush	get home	have a break	pop into
buy	get up	have a shower	read
catch	go to	leave home	set
eat	go to bed	lie	start work
fall asleep	goes off	listen to	turn off
find out	have breakfast	meet	wake up
finish	have dinner	phone	watch TV
get dressed	have lunch		

I usually (1)_____ at 7.00 when my alarm clock (2)_____. I (3)_____ it _____ straight away and then usually just (4)_____ there in bed for another five or ten minutes before I finally (5)_____.I go to the bathroom, (6)_____, (7)_____ my teeth and then (8)_____.

I usually (9)_____ – cornflakes, toast, a boiled egg and coffee – at about 7.40. While I (10)_____ I normally (11)_____ the news on the radio.

I (12)_____ at about 7.50. I always (13)_____ Mr Brown the newsagent's on my way to the station to (14)_____ a daily newspaper. I (15)_____ the eight o'clock train to work and usually (16)_____ the newspaper on it.

I (17)_____ at 9.00 and (18)_____ at 5.00. At eleven o'clock we (19)_____ for tea or coffee and I always (20)_____ at 12.30 – I usually go with some friends to an Italian restaurant just round the corner.

I (21)_____ from work at about six o'clock and
(22)_____ at 7.00. Most evenings I stay at home and
(23)_____. Sometimes, I (24)_____ my
friends at the pub or (25)_____ the cinema. Twice a
week I (26)_____ my mother for a chat and to
(27)_____ how everyone is.

I nearly always (28)_____ at 11.00 or 11.15 on
weekdays, and the last thing I do before I (29)_____ is
to (30)_____ the alarm clock for the next day.

Verbs you can use to talk about your life

Look at the drawings of Peter Steele's life. Write the correct verb under each drawing. Use the past simple tense of each verb.

be born	get divorced	live by the seaside
be buried	get engaged	meet his future wife
become a grandfather	get married	move
buy a house	go to university	remarry
die	have children	retire
fall in love	learn to drive	start school
get a new job	leave school	start work

1 _____

2 _____

3 _____

4 _____

5 _____

6 _____

10

1946

1947

1948

7 _____

8 _____

9 _____

1950

1951–1953

1953

10 _____

11 _____

12 _____

1966

1966

1977

13 _____

14 _____

15 _____

1978

16 _____

1982

17 _____

1985

18 _____

1985–1993

19 _____

1993

20 _____

1993

21 _____

Describing people: Clothes 1

Look at the drawings below and write the correct numbers 1–20 next to the following words.

boxer shorts	pyjamas	suit	trainers
briefs/	raincoat/mac	swimming	umbrella
underpants	shirt	trunks	vest
jacket	shoes	T-shirt	waistcoat
jeans	slippers	tie	
jumper	socks	tracksuit	

Describing people: Clothes 2

Look at the drawings below and write the correct numbers 1–20 next to the following words.

belt	cardigan	handbag	stockings
blouse	coat	hat	sweater
boots	dress	nightdress	swimsuit
bra	dressing-gown	scarf	tights
briefs/knickers	gloves	skirt	trousers

14

Describing people: Physical appearance

1 *The following words can be used to describe people. Put them under the correct heading.*

about 165 cm	fat	short
about twenty-five,	grey	slim
forty, etc.	has a good figure	tall
adult	has freckles	teenager
baby	in his twenties,	thin
bald	fifties, etc.	wavy
blonde, fair	long, short	wears glasses
child	middle-aged	well-built
curly	of average height	well-dressed
dark	old	young
elderly		

Age	Height	Figure/build
Hair	**Other words**	

15

2 *Match the following descriptions with the correct drawing / photo. Write the person's name under the drawing / photo.*

Paul is tall and slim with blonde hair. He's about twenty-five and is wearing a suit.

Mandy is in her thirties and is rather fat. She has dark, curly hair and is well-dressed.

Emma is middle-aged and is about 162 cm tall. She has short, wavy, blonde hair and wears glasses. She is slim and is wearing a dress.

Pamela is about twenty-four and is of average height. She has a good figure and has long, dark hair. She is wearing a jumper, jeans and a pair of boots.

Ken is middle-aged and is of average height. He is well-built with short, dark hair. He is wearing a suit.

Brian is an elderly man who is short and fat. He is bald and wears glasses. He is wearing a jacket.

Timothy is a teenager with short, curly, dark hair. He is about 160 cm tall and has freckles. He is wearing a jumper, jeans and a pair of trainers.

Caroline is about seventeen with short, blonde hair. She is very tall and thin and is wearing a short skirt and a blouse.

1 _____

2 _____

3 _____

4 _____

5 _____

6 _____

7 _____

8 _____

Describing people: Character

1 *Here are twelve adjectives to describe a person's character. Match them with the correct definition below. Write the numbers 1–12 next to each adjective.*

beautiful	happy	lazy	polite
generous	hard-working	mean	rude
handsome	intelligent	miserable	stupid

1 He looks like a film-star. Every girl in the office wants to go out with him. He is very _____.

2 She finds it very easy to learn things and has passed all her exams. She is extremely _____.

3 She is always buying things for people. She is very _____.

4 He hates working and would prefer to stay at home all day in front of the television. He is so _____.

5 He doesn't know anything. He can't even add up two and four. He is so _____.

6 The children next-door are so _____. They never say 'Please' or 'Thank you' and always shout back at their parents.

7 He is always smiling and thinks life is wonderful. He seems to be really _____.

8 He starts work at 6.00 every day and often works overtime or at weekends. He is really _____.

9 She works as a model. When she walks into a room every man turns and stares at her. She is really _____.

10 He hates spending money and never buys anyone a drink at the pub. He is so _____.

11 She always says 'Please' and 'Thank you'. She is a very _____ child.

12 She never has a smile on her face and always looks unhappy. She is so _____.

2 *Here are ten more adjectives to describe a person's character. Again, match them with the correct definition below. Write the numbers 1–10 next to each adjective.*

ambitious	impatient	selfish	sociable
boring	jealous	shy	tidy
imaginative	patient		

1 Everything is always in the right place in his room and on his desk. He is really _____.
2 She finds it very easy to make up stories to tell her children, and can always think of new ideas. She is so _____.
3 He only ever thinks of himself. He is really _____.
4 She wants to get a top job one day and even talks about becoming Prime Minister. She is extremely _____.
5 He hates waiting for people or trains and can't stand it when things don't happen immediately. He is very _____.
6 He loves going to parties and meeting people. He is very _____.
7 The only thing she ever talks about is golf. I almost fell asleep listening to her. She is so _____!
8 He never shouts at us and will explain things over and over again until we understand them. He is very _____.
9 She doesn't like meeting strange people and usually feels nervous and uncomfortable at parties. She is extremely _____.
10 She gets very angry if her husband looks at or dances with another woman. She is extremely _____.

3 *Look at the twenty-two adjectives again and decide whether they are positive or negative. Put them under one of the following headings, then compare your answers with those of someone else.*

Positive characteristics

_____

_____

_____

_____

_____

_____

_____

_____

_____

_____

Negative characteristics

_____

_____

_____

_____

_____

_____

_____

_____

_____

_____

Nationalities

Write the correct nationality under each of the drawings below.
Choose from the following:

American	Chinese	Greek	Scottish
Australian	Dutch	Italian	Spanish
Belgian	English	Japanese	Swedish
Brazilian	French	Russian	Swiss
Canadian	German	Saudi Arabian	Turkish

1 He's _____

2 He's _____

3 He's _____

4 He's _____

5 She's _____

6 He's _____

7 She's _____

8 He's _____

9 She's _____

10 He's_____   11 She's_____   12 He's_____

13 She's_____   14 She's_____   15 She's_____

16 He's_____   17 She's_____   18 He's_____

19 He's_____   20 He's_____

22

Useful phrases

Match the phrases or situations 1–10 with the correct responses a–j.

1 How do you do.

2 How are you?

3 It's my birthday today.

4 I've just got married.

5 (*Someone sneezes.*)

6 Thank you very much.

7 I'm sorry I'm late.

8 I'm taking my driving test tomorrow.

9 Have a nice weekend.

10 (*You step on someone's foot.*)

a Not at all.

b Oh, sorry!

c That's all right.

d How do you do.

e Thank you. The same to you.

f Bless you!

g Many happy returns!

h Good luck!

i Congratulations!

j Fine, thanks. And you?

Write your answers here.

1	2	3	4	5	6	7	8	9	10

Section Two:
House and home

Places to live

Look at the drawings below and write the correct numbers 1–10 next to the following words.

block of flats   detached house   houseboat
bungalow   flat   semi-detached house
caravan   hotel   terraced house
cottage

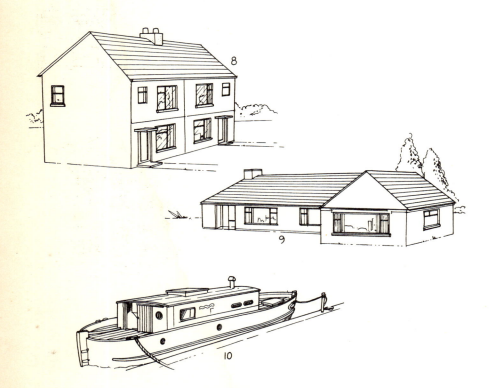

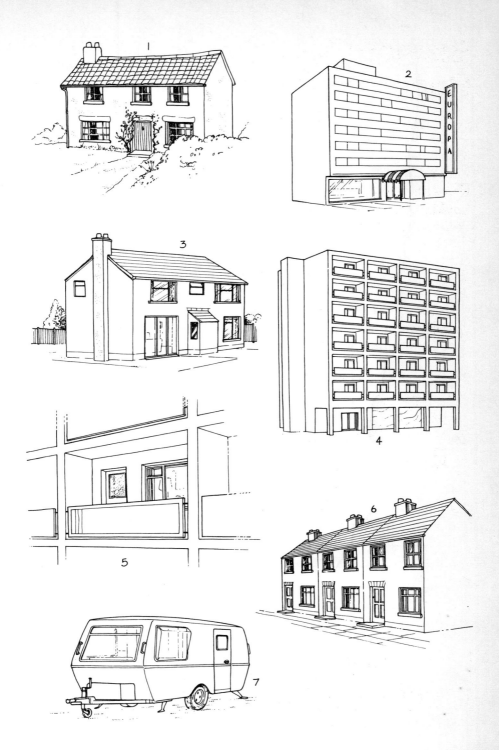

1

2

3

4

5

6

7

EUROPA

Inside a house

*Read the following text and study the drawings on the opposite page. When you have finished, write the words in **bold type** in the text next to the correct numbers 1–14.*

I live in quite a big detached house. Downstairs there are four rooms altogether. As you come in through the **front door**, the first thing you see is a very big **hall**. At the end of the hall is a **staircase** leading upstairs. The first room on the right is the **dining-room**. Opposite this, on the left, is quite a large **living-room**. A door from the living-room leads to a small **study**. Opposite the study, next to the dining-room, is the **kitchen**. This is very big and very modern. It's one of our favourite rooms.

Upstairs there are three bedrooms. As you walk along the **landing** towards the front of the house, there are two bedrooms on your right and one on your left. **Bedroom 1** is very large and has a **balcony** which overlooks the garden. We often have breakfast here in the summer. **Bedroom 2** is in the front of the house and the third bedroom, which we use as a **spare room**, is opposite the **bathroom**. At the end of the landing, on the left, is a separate **toilet**.

Write the words here.

1 _____	8 _____
2 _____	9 _____
3 _____	10 _____
4 _____	11 _____
5 _____	12 _____
6 _____	13 _____
7 _____	14 _____

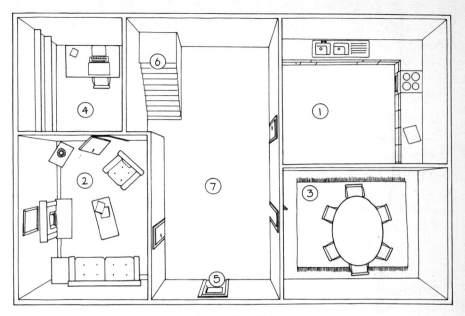

DOWNSTAIRS

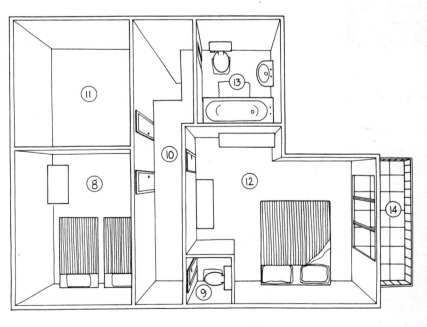

UPSTAIRS

27

Outside a house

*Read the following text and study the drawings on the opposite page. When you have finished, write the words in **bold type** in the text next to the correct numbers 1–20.*

I think the front of my house is very attractive. The **front garden** is full of flowers and bushes, and around the house is a high **hedge**. There's a NO PARKING sign on the **gate** and quite a wide **drive** leading up to the **garage**. From the gate to the garage is a low, brick **wall**.

The **back garden** is very large. At the bottom are several **fruit trees** and a **lawn** with a small **pond** in the middle of it. There is another lawn which comes up to the **patio**. There is also a **flower bed** near the **back door** and a **path** that leads to the **garden shed** and the **greenhouse**, where we grow our own tomatoes. Between our house and our neighbour's is a wooden **fence**.

The only thing I don't like about the house is the **roof**. The **chimney** is very ugly, especially with an **aerial** attached to it. I wish someone would design an attractive television aerial!

Write the words here.

1 _____	11 _____
2 _____	12 _____
3 _____	13 _____
4 _____	14 _____
5 _____	15 _____
6 _____	16 _____
7 _____	17 _____
8 _____	18 _____
9 _____	19 _____
10 _____	20 _____

FRONT

BACK

29

Rooms of a house: The kitchen

Look at the drawing below and write the correct numbers 1–20 next to the following words.

cooker/stove	forks	knives	sink
cupboard	freezer	oven	spoons
cups	fridge	plates	tap
dishwasher	frying pan	saucepan	tea towel
drawer	glasses	shelf	waste bin

Rooms of a house: The living-room

Look at the drawing below and write the correct numbers 1–18 next to the following words.

armchair	curtains	lampshade	sofa
bookcase	cushion	mantelpiece	stereo
carpet	fire	painting	television/TV
ceiling	fireplace	plant	wallpaper
coffee table	lamp		

Rooms of a house: The bathroom

Look at the drawing below and write the correct numbers 1–20 next to the following words.

bar of soap	floor	shampoo	toothbrush
bath	light switch	shower	towel
bath mat	mirror	tiles	tube of
bathroom cabinet	plug	toilet	toothpaste
comb	scales	toilet paper	wash-basin
electric razor			

Rooms of a house: The bedroom

Look at the drawing below and write the correct numbers 1–18 next to the following words.

alarm clock	brush	hair dryer	radiator
bed	chest of drawers	mattress	rug
bedside table	coat hanger	pillow	sheet
bedspread	dressing-table	pillowcase	wardrobe
blanket	duvet		

Jobs and activities in the home

Write the correct verb under each of the drawings below. Choose from the following:

bake a cake	do the gardening	do the washing-up
clean the windows	do the hoovering	lay the table
decorate	do the ironing	make the bed(s)
do the cooking	do the polishing	sweep the floor
do the dusting	do the washing	tidy up

1 _____   2 _____   3 _____

4 _____   5 _____   6 _____

7 _____

8 _____

9 _____

10 _____

11 _____

12 _____

13 _____   14 _____

15 _____

Things in the home

Here is a list of twenty things found in most homes. Look at the drawings below, then write the correct numbers 1–20 next to each of the following words:

ashtray	screwdriver
bottle opener	spanner
bucket	tape measure
cassette recorder	tin opener
corkscrew	toaster
electric iron	torch
hammer	tray
key	vacuum cleaner
pair of scissors	vase
radio	video recorder/VCR

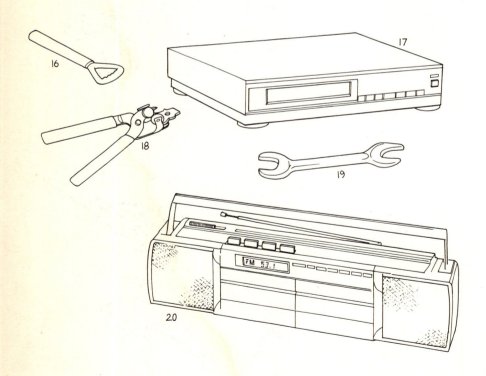

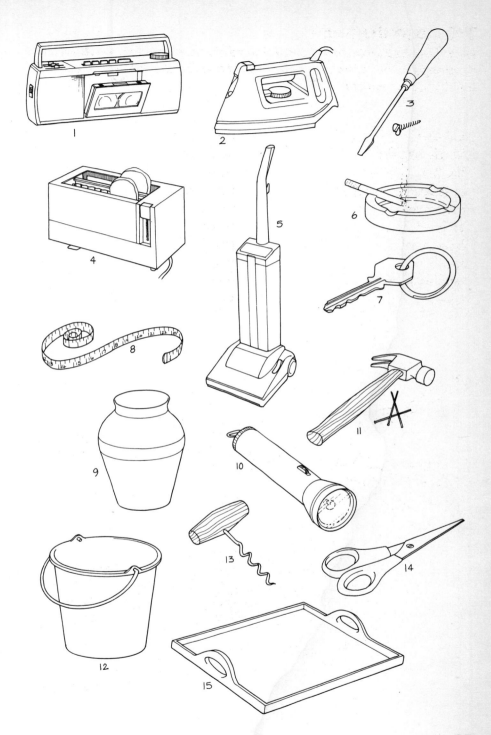

1

2

3

4

5

6

7

8

9

10

11

12

13

14

15

Useful phrases

Match the phrases or situations 1–10 with the correct responses a–j.

1 (*It is 25th December.*)

2 Do you mind if I smoke?

3 I've failed my driving test.

4 Hi!

5 (*It is midnight on 31st December.*)

6 May I take my coat off?

7 (*Someone steals your bag.*)

8 I'm off now, then.

9 Would you like to go to the cinema tonight?

10 (*You want someone to smile for a photograph.*)

a Hi!

b Stop, thief!

c Yes, I'd love to.

d Happy New Year!

e Say 'Cheese'!

f No, not at all.

g Merry Christmas!

h Oh, hard luck!

i Bye, Paul. See you soon.

j Yes, please do.

Write your answers here.

1	2	3	4	5	6	7	8	9	10

Section Three: Jobs, sport and leisure

Jobs 1

Look at the drawings below and on the next two pages and write the correct numbers 1–20 next to the following words.

actor/actress
architect
bricklayer
butcher
dustman
estate agent
fireman
lawyer
librarian
lorry driver

mechanic
nurse
optician
policeman/policewoman
postman
shop assistant
traffic warden
travel agent
vet
waiter/waitress

Who does what?

Using the words from Jobs 1, write the missing words in the following sentences.

1 A _____ tries to put out fires in shops, houses, etc.

2 A _____ helps you with legal problems, e.g. if you want to get divorced or make a will.

3 A _____ cares for people who are ill. He or she usually works in a hospital.

4 A _____ serves you in a shop.

5 A _____ helps you book a journey or a holiday.

6 An _____ designs new buildings.

7 A _____ collects people's rubbish – which is usually in a dustbin.

8 A _____ drives a lorry.

9 A _____ tries to stop people breaking the law.

10 A _____ serves you in a restaurant.

11 An _____ works in the theatre, in films and on television.

12 A _____ is a shopkeeper who sells and cuts up meat.

13 A _____ repairs cars.

14 A _____ makes sure you don't park your car for too long or in the wrong place.

15 A _____ builds houses, etc.

16 An _____ checks people's eyes and also sells glasses.

17 A _____ is a doctor who treats sick or injured animals.

18 An _____ helps you buy or sell your house or flat.

19 A _____ works in a library.

20 A _____ delivers letters and parcels to your home.

Jobs 2

Look at the drawings below and on the next two pages and write the correct numbers 1–20 next to the following words.

baker	farmer
barber/hairdresser	journalist/reporter
businessman/businesswoman	musician
carpenter	photographer
cleaner	pilot
computer programmer	plumber
cook	secretary
dentist	soldier
doctor	surgeon
electrician	teacher

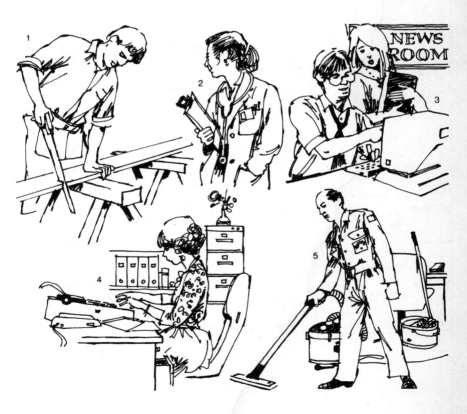

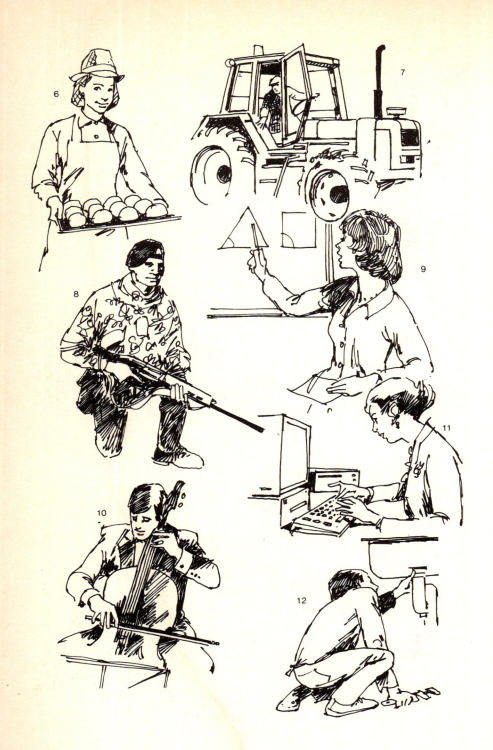

Who uses what?

Here is the list of jobs from Jobs 2 again. See if you can work out who uses what. Choose from the items a–t on the right. Use each word once only.

1	baker	a	briefcase
2	barber/hairdresser	b	drill, mouth mirror
3	businessman/businesswoman	c	notebook
4	carpenter	d	spanner, pipes
5	cleaner	e	blackboard
6	computer programmer	f	saw, wood
7	cook	g	oven
8	dentist	h	stethoscope
9	doctor	i	camera
10	electrician	j	gun
11	farmer	k	vacuum cleaner
12	journalist/reporter	l	tractor
13	musician	m	joystick
14	photographer	n	comb, scissors
15	pilot	o	typewriter, word processor
16	plumber	p	scalpel
17	secretary	q	computer
18	soldier	r	screwdriver
19	surgeon	s	musical instrument
20	teacher	t	frying pan, saucepan

Write your answers here.

1	2	3	4	5	6	7	8	9	10	11	12	13	14	15	16	17	18	19	20

Adjectives you can use to describe a job

Here are twelve adjectives you can use to describe a job. Look up any words you do not understand in your dictionary. Try to write next to each word one or two jobs. You can use the words from Jobs 1–2 or any other jobs you can think of. When you have finished, compare your answers with those of someone else in the class.

badly paid		
boring		
clean		
creative		
dangerous		
dead-end		
dirty		
exciting		
skilled		
stressful		
unskilled		
unsuitable for a man		
unsuitable for a woman		
well-paid		

In an office

Look at the drawing below and write the correct numbers 1–20 next to the following words.

blind	drawing pin	printer
calculator	fax machine	rubber
calendar	file	stapler
chair	filing cabinet	telephone
computer/PC	hole punch	typewriter
desk	paper clip	wastepaper basket
diary	photocopier	

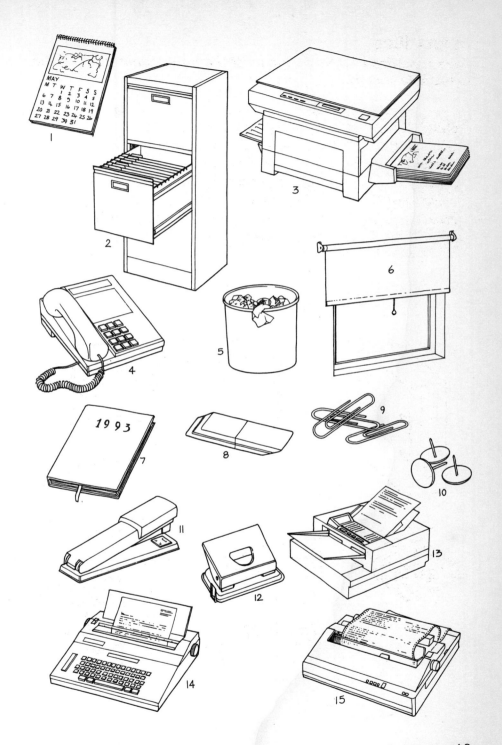

Places where you play or do sports

Look at the drawings below and write underneath each one what it is called. Choose from the words below. Use a word from the left with a word from the right. The first one has been done for you.

boxing	rink
football	course
golf	court
ice	pitch
running	pool
ski	track
swimming	slope
tennis	ring

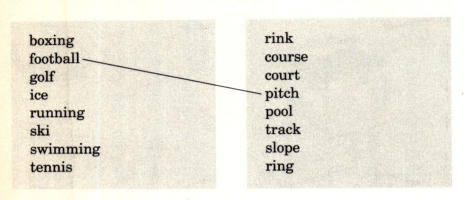

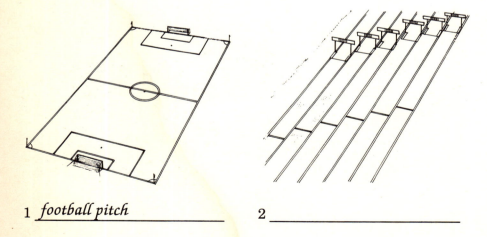

1 *football pitch*

2 _____

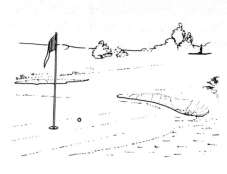

3 _____

4 _____

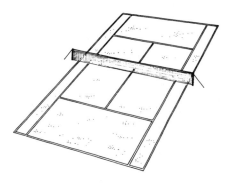

5 _____

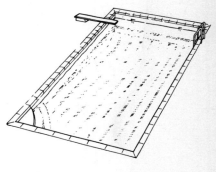

6 _____

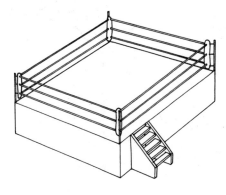

7 _____

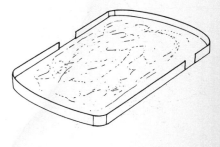

8 _____

Popular sports

Look at the drawings and write the correct numbers 1–20 next to the following words.

athletics	cycling	motor racing	squash
badminton	gymnastics	rugby	table tennis
basketball	hockey	sailing	weight-lifting
boxing	horse-racing	show-jumping	windsurfing
cricket	ice skating	snooker	wrestling

What do you use?

The following drawings are of pieces of sports equipment. Match them with the correct sport on the next page. Write the pieces of equipment a–l next to the correct word.

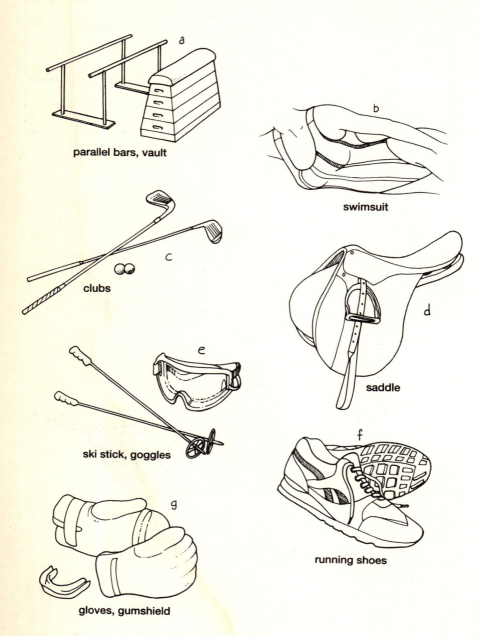

parallel bars, vault

swimsuit

clubs

saddle

ski stick, goggles

running shoes

gloves, gumshield

Sport	Equipment used	Sport	Equipment used
athletics		horse-racing	
badminton, tennis		ice skating	
boxing		skiing	
cricket		snooker	
golf		swimming	
gymnastics		weight-lifting	

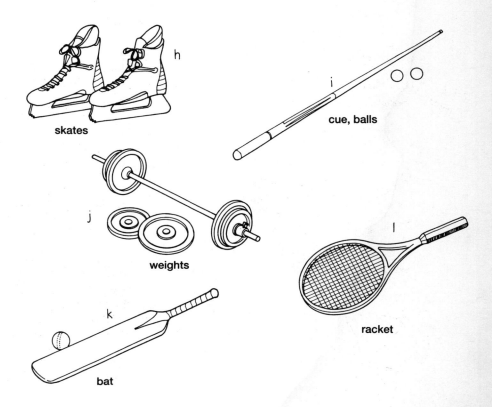

h skates

i cue, balls

j weights

k bat

l racket

Hobbies and pastimes

Look at the drawings and write the correct numbers 1–20 next to the following words.

aerobics	fishing	playing cards
bird-watching	gardening	playing chess
camping	going to evening	playing the piano
cooking	classes	pottery
cycling	jogging	reading
dancing	knitting	stamp collecting
dressmaking	photography	watching TV

What are they called and where do you use them?

1 *Look at the drawings below of things used with various hobbies or pastimes and write the correct numbers 1–12 next to the following words.*

bicycle	leotard	remote control
binoculars	magnifying glass	scissors, tape measure
camera	needles, wool	spade, wellingtons
fishing rod	recipe, frying pan	tent

2 *Now say which hobbies or pastimes would use the things on the previous page. Choose from the ones on pages 56–7. Write your answers here.*

1 _____   7 _____

2 _____   8 _____

3 _____   9 _____

4 _____   10 _____

5 _____   11 _____

6 _____   12 _____

Useful phrases

Match the phrases or situations 1–10 with the correct responses a–j.

1 Hello. My name's Peter.

2 Did you have a good trip?

3 (*Someone hits the ball into the net in tennis.*)

4 I'm going to bed now.

5 Is anyone sitting here?

6 Goodbye.

7 I'm off to a party tonight.

8 Another cup of tea, James?

9 I'm going to Paris at the weekend.

10 (*Someone is standing in front of you and you want to pass.*)

a   Goodbye. It was nice meeting you.

b   Have a good trip.

c   Good night. Sleep well.

d   Excuse me, please.

e   Hello. I'm Julia.

f   Have a nice time!

g   Yes, pretty good, thanks.

h   No, of course not.

i   Yes, please.

j   Oh, bad luck!

Write your answers here.

1	2	3	4	5	6	7	8	9	10

Check 1

This is a check to see how many words you can remember from Section One, Section Two and Section Three. Try to do it without looking back at the previous pages.

1 He's my brother's son. He's my _____.
   (a) niece   (b) cousin   (c) nephew   (d) uncle

2 Which of the following is part of the face?
   (a) heel   (b) cushion   (c) thigh   (d) cheek

3 Which of the following parts of the body is found below the waist?
   (a) ankle   (b) chest   (c) elbow   (d) throat

4 Which of the following do you wear under a shirt?
   (a) mac   (b) vest   (c) waistcoat   (d) scarf

5 Which of the following are not usually worn by a man?
   (a) socks   (b) slippers   (c) boxer shorts   (d) tights

6 He hates spending money. He's very _____.
   (a) lazy   (b) patient   (c) mean   (d) selfish

7 A house with all the rooms on the same floor is called a_____.
   (a) cottage   (b) terraced house   (c) semi-detached house
   (d) bungalow

8 In which room of a house would you usually find a wash-basin?
   (a) the bathroom   (b) the kitchen   (c) the study
   (d) the living-room

9 Which of the following is usually found in the bedroom?
   (a) coffee table   (b) dressing-table   (c) sofa   (d) sink

10 Which person works with animals?
   (a) a bricklayer   (b) a lawyer   (c) a carpenter   (d) a vet

11 In each of the following groups of four words, one does not fit in. <u>Underline</u> the word and try to say why it is different from the rest.

  (a) aunt, sister, son, granddaughter

  (b) blouse, skirt, stockings, underpants

  (c) fence, landing, patio, greenhouse

  (d) dustman, policeman, soldier, pilot

  (e) rugby, boxing, football, snooker

12 There are thirteen words hidden in the following word square. They are all things found in the home. See how many you can find. You can read vertically (5 words), horizontally (5 words) or diagonally (3 words).

```
A  D  S  C  R  E  W  D  R  I  V  E  R  B  S  H
C  T  K  D  F  R  T  G  O  J  E  C  E  L  C  Y
R  O  I  K  A  L  T  B  R  H  O  W  S  T  I  U
T  A  C  J  E  O  H  G  A  S  Q  L  P  E  S  A
G  S  W  D  I  Y  E  S  D  V  B  H  A  J  S  T
O  T  S  H  F  I  S  A  I  F  A  C  N  U  O  B
T  E  M  C  T  R  A  Y  O  K  V  S  N  L  R  U
S  R  I  D  O  N  K  Q  V  I  D  W  E  C  S  C
P  M  L  P  B  A  C  N  E  G  E  N  R  C  A  K
V  A  C  C  U  M  C  L  E  A  N  E  R  J  H  E
D  S  R  I  T  R  H  I  T  P  O  B  C  D  U  T
B  H  A  P  G  O  R  V  H  A  M  M  E  R  K  L
W  T  D  C  B  A  R  N  D  F  Y  I  H  I  B  J
A  R  E  G  R  D  Q  C  O  R  K  S  C  R  E  W
B  A  V  M  C  D  H  N  H  E  B  A  K  T  L  P
S  Y  T  A  P  E  M  E  A  S  U  R  E  M  I  A
```

13 Read through the following sentences and try to work out what the missing words are. To help you, the first and last letters of the words are given.

  (a) David is my Christian name and Watson my s_____e.

  (b) I usually c__h the 8.30 bus to work.

  (c) I'm going to bed. Do you know where my p_____s are?

  (d) She loves meeting people. She's very s_____e.

(e) I live on the tenth floor of that b___k of f___s over there.

(f) Come and stay with us for Christmas. You can sleep in the s___e r___m.

(g) There was a high f___e all around the house.

(h) The cups and plates are in the c_____d.

(i) The carpet's dirty. I really must do the h_____g tomorrow.

(j) She makes sure you don't park your car in the wrong place. She's a t_____c w____n.

14 Look at the family tree below. Then read through the sentences and write the missing names in the boxes.

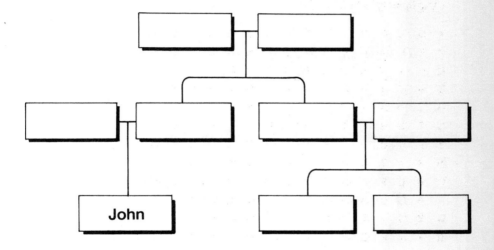

- Sandra's brother is called Roger.
- Rebecca and Emily are sisters.
- Mary met her husband, Albert, at a Christmas party.
- Roger and Doreen got married in 1984.
- Roger is John's uncle.
- Albert and Mary have two children – Sandra and Roger.
- Emily is John's cousin.
- Mary and Albert have three grandchildren – John, Emily and Rebecca.
- John's parents are called David and Sandra.
- Rebecca's grandparents are called Albert and Mary.

15 Match the words on the left with the words on the right. Draw lines between the correct pairs.

athletics	bat
bird-watching	shower
kitchen	racket
cricket	needles
reporter	spanner
gymnastics	fridge
bathroom	running track
tennis	vault
knitting	notebook
plumber	binoculars

16 Say whether the following sentences are true (T) or false (F).

(a) I'm **single** and my wife's name is Susan.

(b) Your **forehead** is above your eyes.

(c) You usually wear a **bra** on your feet.

(d) He hates waiting. He's very **ambitious**.

(e) These clothes are dirty. I'd better do the **washing-up** tomorrow.

(f) He cuts men's hair. He's a **barber**.

(g) An optician often wears a **leotard** at work.

(h) I get lots of money. My job is really **well-paid**.

(i) The boxer picked up his **cue** before he stepped into the ring.

(j) Jogging and aerobics help to keep me **slim**.

17 The following sentences describe the life of Pamela Bates. Put them in the right order. Mark them 1–10.

She met her husband on holiday in July 1964.   ____

She started school at the age of five.   ____

She got divorced in 1989.   ____

She moved to Brighton when she was forty.   ____

She left school in 1963.   ____

She retired last year and now lives alone in a
two-roomed flat.

Her first child was born in 1970. ____

She got married when she was twenty-one. ____

She was born in 1944. ____

She started work a month after she left school. ____

18 Look at the two drawings, then write the missing words in the
descriptions below. To help you, the first letter of each missing
word is given.

(a) He is a t_____, s_____,
y_____ man. He has
l_____, d_____,
c_____ hair and is wearing a
j_____, a striped t_____
and a pair of t_____. He is
holding an u_____ in his
right hand. He finds it very easy
to make up stories for his children
at bedtime. He is really
i_____.

(b) She is an e_____ woman of
about _____, with s_____,
g_____ hair. She is quite
s_____ and wears g_____.
She is rather f_____ and is
wearing a dark c_____ and a
s_____. She is holding a
h_____ under her arm. She is
always buying things for her
children and grandchildren. She is
very g_____.

19 Complete the following dialogues (or situations).

    (a) A: How do you do.

        B: H_____

    (b) A: It's my birthday today.

        B: M_____

    (c) A: I've just got married.

        B: C_____

    (d) A: Have a nice weekend.

        B: Thank you. _____

    (e) A: Would you like to go to the cinema tonight?

        B: Yes, _____

    (f)   (*You want someone to smile for a photograph.*)

        B: S_____

    (g)   (*Someone steals your bag.*)

        B: S_____

    (h) A: Another cup of tea, Pamela?

        B: Y_____

    (i)   (*Someone is standing in front of you and you want to pass.*)

        B: E_____

    (j) A: I'm going to Paris at the weekend.

        B: H_____

20 Here are thirty words in alphabetical order. Place each word under the correct heading. (Five words under each.)

waist	hole punch	photocopier	tap
camping	jaw	photography	tea towel
cheek	knee	pottery	thumb
chin	lip	saucepan	waste bin
desk	motor racing	shoulder	wrestling
dressmaking	nose	show-jumping	wrist
filing cabinet	oven	squash	
hockey	paper clip	stamp collecting	

In the kitchen

_____

_____

_____

_____

_____

In the office

_____

_____

_____

_____

_____

Parts of the face

_____

_____

_____

_____

_____

Parts of the body

_____

_____

_____

_____

_____

Popular sports

_____

_____

_____

_____

_____

Popular hobbies

_____

_____

_____

_____

_____

21 Look at the drawings and complete the crossword. Each of the missing words is a different nationality.

Across →

 1
 10
 3
 14
 4
 15
 6
 16
 7

Down ↓

 2
 9
 3
 11
 5
 12
 7
 13
 8

69

Section Four:
Food, shops and shopping

Things we use in the kitchen

Look at the drawings below and write the correct numbers 1–15 next to the following words.

apron	grater	microwave	scales
bottle opener	grill	oven glove	tin opener
bowl	jug	rolling pin	toaster
frying pan	kettle	saucepan	

Verbs to do with cooking

Here are eight verbs to do with cooking.

| bake | chop | grate | mash |
| boil | fry | grill | roast |

Put the correct verb in front of the following.

1 _____ some pork chops (*under the grill*)
2 _____ pork or beef (*in the oven*)
3 _____ potatoes (*in a saucepan with a fork*)
4 _____ bread or a cake (*in the oven*)
5 _____ bacon or sausages (*in a frying pan*)
6 _____ cheese (*with a grater*)
7 _____ meat or carrots (*with a knife*)
8 _____ an egg, water (*in a saucepan*)

How to make a good cup of tea

In the following text on how to make a good cup of tea, the lines are in the wrong order. Put them in the correct order 1–12. Number 1 has been done for you.

some of the water into a teapot to heat it	___
and one for the pot. Take the teapot to	___
put the lid on the teapot and let it brew	___
Fill a kettle full of cold water. Let the	1
the kettle and pour the water on to the	___
a perfect cup of tea.	___
go on boiling for very long. Pour	___
put in the tea, one teaspoon per person	___
tea while it is still boiling. Stir briskly,	___
thoroughly. Pour the water away and	___
water come to the boil, but do not let it	___
for several minutes. You will now have	___

Fruit, nuts and berries

Look at the drawings below and write the correct numbers 1–18 next to the following words.

apple	coconut	nuts	plum
avocado	grapefruit	orange	rhubarb
banana	grapes	peach	strawberry
blackberry	lemon	pear	
cherry	melon	pineapple	

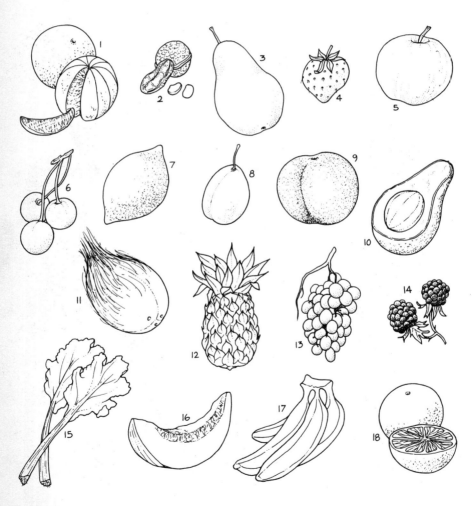

Vegetables

Look at the drawings below and write the correct numbers 1–20 next to the following words.

asparagus	cauliflower	green/red	onion
beans	celery	peppers	parsley
beetroot	corn on the cob	leek	peas
Brussels sprout	cucumber	lettuce	radish
cabbage	garlic	mushroom	tomato
carrot			

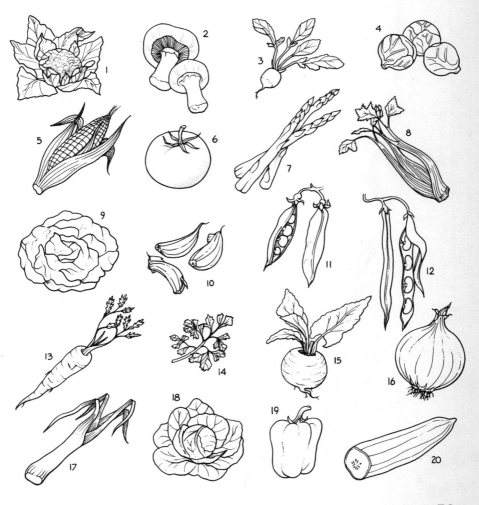

Groceries

Look at the drawings below and write the correct numbers 1–24 next to the following words.

bacon	coke	milk	sausages
biscuits	cornflakes	mineral water	soup
bread	crisps	pie	spaghetti
butter	eggs	rice	sweets
cakes	fish	roast chicken	tea-bags
chips	meat	rolls	yoghurt

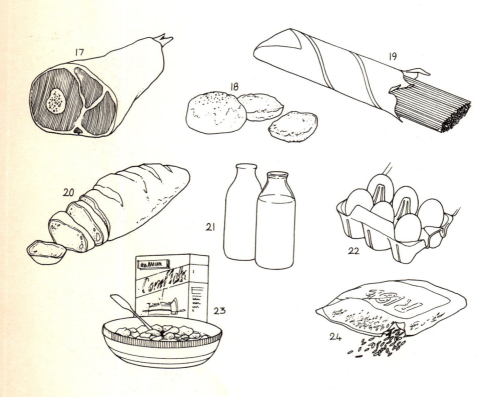

How we buy groceries

Match the words 1–15 on the left with the groceries a–o on the right.

1 a bar of	a orange juice, yoghurt
2 a bottle of	b bread
3 a box of	c margarine
4 a bunch of	d milk
5 a can of	e chocolate, soap
6 a carton of	f jam, marmalade
7 a dozen	g apples, potatoes, oranges
8 a jar/pot of	h wine, mineral water, shampoo
9 a joint of	i eggs
10 a loaf of	j soup, sardines, cat food
11 a packet of	k matches, chocolates
12 a pint/litre of	l beer, coke
13 a pound/kilo of	m biscuits, cornflakes, cigarettes
14 a tin of	n meat
15 a tub of	o grapes, bananas, flowers

Write your answers here.

1	2	3	4	5	6	7	8	9	10	11	12	13	14	15

Shops and shopping

Write the missing shops or buildings in the sentences below. Choose from the following:

baker's	fishmonger's	off-licence
bank	florist's	post office
barber's	furniture shop	record shop
butcher's	greengrocer's	shoe shop
café	hairdresser's	supermarket
card shop	ironmonger's	tobacconist's
chemist's	jeweller's	toy shop
department store	launderette	
dry cleaner's	newsagent's	

1 You can buy birthday cards and Christmas cards at the

   _____.

2 You can buy a new sofa or a bed at the _____.

3 You can buy newspapers and magazines at the

   _____.

4 You can buy cigarettes, matches and cigars at the

   _____.

5 You can buy bread and cakes at the _____.

6 You can buy almost everything at Harrods in London. It is a
   very big _____.

7 Men can get their hair cut at the _____ and women
   at the _____.

8 You can buy stamps and post letters and parcels at the

   _____.

9 You can buy fish at the _____.

10 You can cash a cheque and borrow money at the

   _____.

11 You can buy fruit and vegetables at the _____.

12 You can buy a bottle of wine or whisky to take home with you at the _____.

13 You can buy a jigsaw puzzle or a doll's house at the _____.

14 You can buy medicine, make-up or perfume at the _____.

15 You can buy a hammer and a screwdriver at the _____.

16 You can buy CDs, records or cassettes at the _____.

17 You can get your clothes cleaned at the _____.

18 You can do the weekly shopping for food at the _____.

19 You can buy meat and sausages at the _____.

20 You can buy a pair of boots or slippers at the _____.

21 You can wash your dirty clothes at the _____.

22 You can have a cup of coffee and a sandwich at the _____.

23 You can buy a bunch of roses at the _____.

24 You can buy a ring or a watch at the _____.

At a restaurant

Write the missing words in the menu below. Choose from the following:

apple pie and custard
boiled potatoes
chips
duck with orange sauce
fillet of plaice

fruit cocktail
lamb chops
prawn cocktail
runner beans
tomato soup

Starters

melon

pâté with toast

1_____

grapefruit

2_____

Main course   Vegetables

3_____ 6_____

roast beef   7_____

sirloin steak

4_____   *jacket potatoes*

mushrooms

roast lamb with mint sauce 8_____

5_____   *salad*

Desserts

9_____

cheesecake

chocolate gateau

10_____

strawberry ice-cream

Useful phrases

Match the phrases or situations 1–10 with the correct responses a–j.

1 (*You want to pay for a meal at a restaurant.*)

2 My mother died last week.

3 May I introduce Peter Brown.

4 Have you met Anne?

5 (*Shop assistant in a shop.*) Can I help you?

6 I'm hungry.

7 (*You don't hear or understand something someone says to you.*)

8 Thanks for the party.

9 Could you help me, please?

10 Would you like a drink?

a It's all right, thank you. I'm just looking.

b Yes, certainly.

c Could I have the bill, please?

d No, thank you. I'm driving.

e How do you do.

f I'm glad you enjoyed it.

g I'm so sorry.

h No, I don't think so.

i Sorry?

j Help yourself to a sandwich.

Write your answers here.

1	2	3	4	5	6	7	8	9	10

Section Five:
The world of nature

Months and seasons

1 *Write the name of the season above each of the drawings below.*
Also write the names of the months associated with each season.
Choose from the following:

April	February	March	September
August	January	May	spring
autumn	July	November	summer
December	June	October	winter

	months	**events**

	months	**events**

81

	months	events

	months	events

2 *When do the following events happen? Write them next to the correct season above.*

bonfire night
Christmas
Easter
Hallowe'en
New Year's Eve
Nobel day
Oscar prize-giving ceremony
St Valentine's Day
the longest day of the year
the shortest day of the year
when most people go on
  holiday

when the school year starts
when the school year ends
when the weather is coldest
when the weather is
  warmest
when young animals (e.g.
  lambs) are born
Wimbledon tennis
  championships

What's the weather like?

Look at the drawings below and write down what the weather is like.
Choose from the following:

below zero	foggy	raining	sunny
clearing up	frosty	snowing	very hot
cloudy	misty	stormy	windy

1 It's _____

2 It's _____

3 It's _____

4 It's _____

5 It's _____

6 It's _____

7 It's _____

8 It's _____

9 It's _____

10 It's _____

11 It's _____

12 It's _____

83

Weather forecast

Look at the map of Great Britain, then write the missing words in the weather forecast. Choose from the following:

cloudy with sunny periods	high winds and showers
dry and sunny	rain
dull and overcast	showers and sunny periods
fog and mist patches	snow storms
heavy snow	storms

The north of Scotland will have (1)_____
during most of the day, with temperatures reaching 4 degrees
centigrade. It will be slightly warmer in the south of Scotland
but (2)_____ is expected throughout the day.
The north-west of England will have
(3)_____ – especially over high ground.
North-east England will stay (4)_____ for
most of the day.
(5)_____ are expected in North Wales, while
in South Wales you can expect (6)_____.
The Midlands will be (7)_____, while East
Anglia will have (8)_____. The west of England will have (9)_____ with outbreaks of
thunder and lightning.
Finally, in the south-east of England it will be
(10)_____ all day.

More words to do with the weather

1 *Match the weather words on the left with the correct definitions on the right. Draw lines between them. One has already been done for you.*

a blizzard	dark with a lot of clouds in the sky
a breeze	a short period of rain
a gale	rather cold
a shower	a storm with heavy snow and high winds
changeable	light rain falling in very small drops
chilly	sun and clouds
drizzle	a very strong wind
overcast	heavy rain
pouring	changing from one type of weather to another
sunny spells	a light or gentle wind

2 *Which of the above words best describes the following two drawings?*

Animals 1: Pets and farm animals

Look at the drawings below and write the correct numbers 1–20 next to the following words.

bull	dog	hamster	pig
calf	donkey	hen	puppy
cat	duck	horse	rabbit
cock	goat	kitten	sheep
cow	goose	lamb	tortoise

Animals 2: Wild animals

Look at the drawings below and write the correct numbers 1–20 next to the following words.

bat	fox	monkey	squirrel
bear	giraffe	mouse	tiger
camel	hedgehog	penguin	whale
dolphin	kangaroo	rat	wolf
elephant	lion	shark	zebra

Animals 3: Insects and other animals

Look at the drawings below and write the correct numbers 1–18 next to the following words.

ant	fly	octopus	spider
bee	frog	pigeon	wasp
beetle	ladybird	scorpion	worm
butterfly	mosquito	snail	
crab	moth	snake	

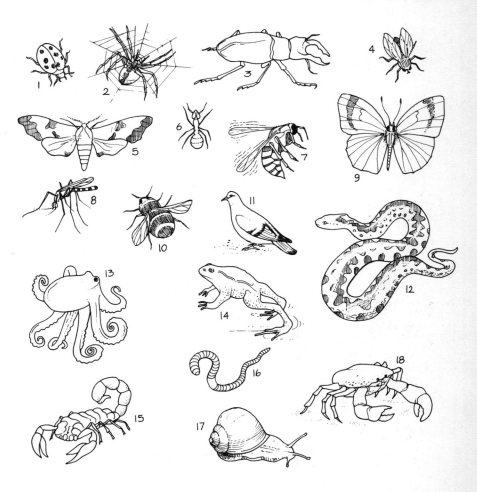

Animal sounds

Match the animals 1–15 on the left with the sounds they make a–o.

1 a bee	a croaks
2 a cat	b squeaks
3 a cock	c hisses
4 a dog	d neighs
5 a donkey	e buzzes
6 a duck	f grunts
7 a frog	g miaows, purrs
8 a hen	h howls
9 a horse	i brays
10 a lion	j bleats
11 a mouse	k clucks
12 a pig	l crows
13 a sheep, a lamb	m roars
14 a snake	n quacks
15 a wolf	o barks

Write your answers here.

1	2	3	4	5	6	7	8	9	10	11	12	13	14	15

Natural disasters

1 *Write the correct words under the drawings below. Choose from the following:*

avalanche	flood	hurricane
drought	forest fire	volcanic eruption
earthquake		

1 _____ 2 _____ 3 _____

4 _____ 5 _____ 6 _____

7 _____

2 *Now try to work out which of the disasters the following people are talking about.*

(a) 'It's terrible! We haven't had any rain now for over a year. The rivers are almost dry and if we don't get rain soon thousands of people are going to die.'

(b) 'Suddenly the ground started shaking. Next thing, a big gap appeared in the road and the building opposite collapsed. I've never been so frightened in all my life.'

(c) 'We're very lucky to be alive! Two more hours and the whole village would have been covered with hot lava. It's a miracle we managed to get away in time. And to think that we were taking photographs of the volcano just two days before, when everything was so calm and peaceful.'

(d) 'It was our first visit to Florida and of course we'd heard about them before, but it's only when you're there that you see just how strong the winds are and how much damage they can do. My wife saw a whole roof being blown off and a car flying through the air. No, I think we'll stick to Spain next year – it's safer.'

(e) 'The mountain looked all right and the snow seemed very firm when we were skiing. Then suddenly it happened. It felt as if the whole mountain was moving. And the snow came down so quickly. Thank God I'd decided to stop half an hour before it happened. Some others staying at the hotel weren't so lucky. They're still trying to find them underneath all the snow.'

(f) 'The river overflowed its banks. Well, it was bound to happen after so many weeks of rain. There was water everywhere. We had to sit on our roof and wait for someone to rescue us. It was pretty frightening, I can tell you, as the water was rising by a couple of inches every hour.'

(g) 'My friend and I were fishing by a lake when we first spotted it, or rather smelt it. Fortunately, we had a car phone and were able to report it. But it still took a very long time to put out, and nearly half the trees have been destroyed.'

In the countryside

*Read the following text and study the drawing on the next page. When you have finished, write the words in **bold** type in the text next to the correct numbers 1–16.*

The **village** of Stockley lies in a narrow **valley**. In the distance are the high **peaks** of the Black **Mountains**. There is a **wood** near the village and running through it is a **river**. Above the village is a **waterfall** which runs into a small **lake**.

Not far from Stockley is Potter's Farm. A narrow **lane** leads from the farmhouse to the **main road**. Cows are grazing in the large **field** near the farm and there are lots of sheep on the **hills** behind. Some hikers are following the **footpath** to the village. They have just crossed over the tiny **stream** that runs through Potter's Farm, while some farm workers are busy cutting the **hedges** in the **meadow** near the lake.

Write the words here.

1 _____	9 _____
2 _____	10 _____
3 _____	11 _____
4 _____	12 _____
5 _____	13 _____
6 _____	14 _____
7 _____	15 _____
8 _____	16 _____

Useful phrases

Match the phrases or situations 1–10 with the correct responses a–j.

1 (*You open a door for someone to go through.*)

2 Pass the salt, please.

3 (*Someone is looking very unhappy.*)

4 Could I speak to Sarah, please?

5 Pam, this is Brian.

6 (*Someone has bought you a drink at the pub.*)

7 What shall we do tonight?

8 What do you do for a living?

9 Sorry I can't help you.

10 I can't come to the party. I've got to work.

a Hello. Pleased to meet you.

b I'm a teacher.

c How about going to the cinema?

d What a pity!

e After you!

f Cheer up!

g Never mind. Thanks anyway.

h She's out at the moment. Can I take a message?

i Cheers!

j Certainly. Here you are.

Write your answers here.

1	2	3	4	5	6	7	8	9	10

Section Six: Adjectives, verbs and prepositions

Adjectives: Common opposites

Look at the pairs of drawings below and supply the missing adjectives. Choose from the following:

blunt	empty	old	thin
closed/shut	expensive/	short	ugly
dark	dear	slow	unhappy/
difficult	low	small	sad
dirty	narrow	smooth	weak
dry	new	soft	

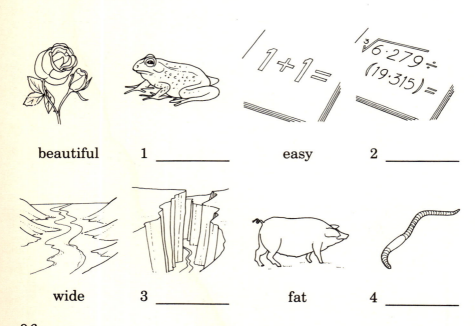

beautiful   1 _____   easy   2 _____

wide   3 _____   fat   4 _____

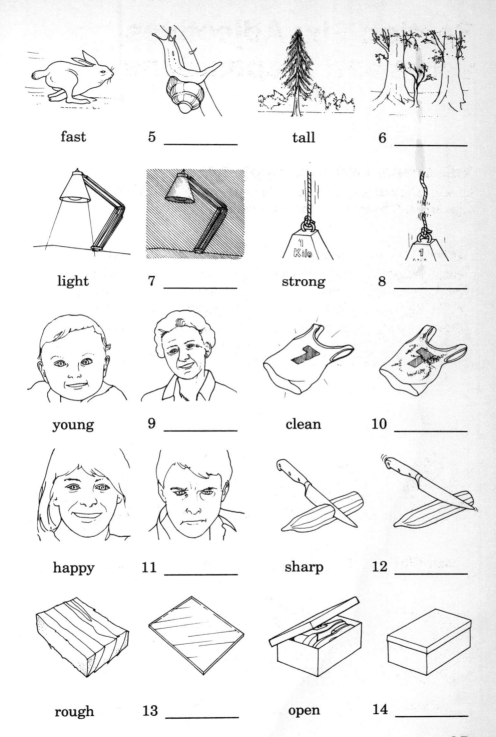

fast   5 _____   tall   6 _____

light   7 _____   strong   8 _____

young   9 _____   clean   10 _____

happy   11 _____   sharp   12 _____

rough   13 _____   open   14 _____

old   15 _____   wet   16 _____

high   17 _____   big, large   18 _____

full   19 _____   hard   20 _____

cheap   21 _____

Useful adjectives 1

Complete each of the sentences below with a suitable adjective. Use each word once only. Choose from the following:

alive	busy	comfortable	free
asleep	careful	deep	funny
brave	clever	famous	hot
bright	cold	foreign	

1 What a _____ armchair! I could easily fall asleep sitting in this.

2 Japanese cars are the most popular _____ cars in this country.

3 Could I open the window, please? It's very _____ in here.

4 He was very _____ and was always top of the class at school.

5 He wasn't killed in the accident. He's still _____.

6 That light is very _____! It's hurting my eyes!

7 Everyone has heard of her. She's very _____.

8 You don't have to pay for it. It's _____.

9 Don't wake her up. She's still _____.

10 She's never had an accident since she started driving. She's a very _____ driver.

11 Be careful! The water is very _____ here.

12 To be a soldier you have to be quite _____.

13 I like watching Charlie Chaplin films. I think they're really _____.

14 Put a jumper on, Colin. It's quite _____ outside.

15 I've got so many things to do this week. I'm going to be very _____.

Useful adjectives 2

Complete each of the sentences below with a suitable adjective. Use each word once only. Choose from the following:

afraid	kind	married	sweet
hungry	late	modern	thirsty
ill	long	rich	tired
important	loud	straight	

1 The train journey took longer than usual, so he arrived ten minutes _____ for his meeting.

2 I'm _____. I think I'll go to bed.

3 Most pop singers and film stars earn a lot of money. It must be nice to be _____ like them.

4 'How _____ is this river?'
  'About 80 miles.'

5 Have you got anything to eat, Julie? I'm _____.

6 'Is David single?'
  'No, he's _____. His wife's name is Geraldine.'

7 Two lumps of sugar, please. I like _____ tea.

8 Leave the light on, please. I'm _____ of the dark!

9 The teacher told her pupils it was _____ to work hard at school and to pass their exams.

10 Which do you prefer – old houses or _____ ones?

11 Turn the radio down, please. It's very _____.

12 He couldn't come to the party because he was _____.

13 If you want to draw _____ lines, you'd better use a ruler.

14 Our neighbours are always helping us. They're very _____.

15 I'm _____. Have you got anything to drink?

Adjectives to describe people and things

Complete the sentences 1–15 on the left with a suitable adjective from the list a–o on the right.

1 A pipe is

2 A feather is

3 A football is

4 A lemon is

5 Homeless people are usually

6 Hitting children or pets is

7 The Empire State Building is

8 2 + 2 = 4. This sum is

9 Drinking alcohol can make you

10 It really happened. The story is

11 A diamond ring is

12 A billiard table is

13 These vegetables are

14 A knife is

15 Glue and jam are

a bitter

b correct

c cruel

d sharp and dangerous

e drunk

f expensive

g flat and smooth

h fresh

i high

j light

k narrow and hollow

l poor

m round

n sticky

o true

Write your answers here.

1	2	3	4	5	6	7	8	9	10	11	12	13	14	15

Verbs that describe activities 1

Look at the drawings below and write the correct numbers 1–20 next to the following verbs.

bite	cry	kiss	smile
blow	draw	laugh	throw
build	dream	shout	watch TV
carry	drink	sit	wave
cough	drive	sleep	write

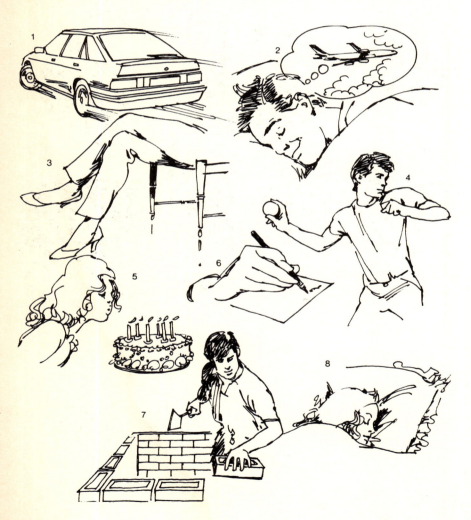

Verbs that describe activities 2

Look at the drawings below and write the correct numbers 1–20 next to the following verbs.

blow one's	die	pay	teach
nose	fight	quarrel	wash one's
climb	fly	run	hair
count	hold	shake hands	yawn
cycle	jump	sneeze	
dance	paint	swim	

Useful verbs 1

Match the verbs 1–15 on the left with a suitable phrase from the list a–o on the right.

1 answer		a	the blackboard
2 bake		b	two languages
3 close		c	a dress, glasses
4 cook		d	the phone, a question
5 cut		e	a pipe, a cigarette, a fire
6 dig		f	a letter
7 fail		g	a story, a lie
8 light		h	a meal
9 look at		i	the guitar, tennis
10 play		j	things with a knife
11 post		k	the light
12 speak		l	a cake
13 switch on/off		m	an exam, a driving test
14 tell		n	a door, a window
15 wear		o	the garden

Write your answers here.

1	2	3	4	5	6	7	8	9	10	11	12	13	14	15

Useful verbs 2

Match the verbs 1–15 on the left with a suitable phrase from the list a–o on the right.

1 ask	a a bicycle, a horse
2 cash	b your name
3 comb	c a club
4 cross	d a question
5 deliver	e on the pavement
6 join	f cigarettes, a pipe
7 knock	g your hair
8 make	h money, two weeks in a place
9 ride	i at a door
10 sing	j a road
11 smoke	k a cheque
12 solve	l a letter, a parcel
13 spell	m a song
14 spend	n tea, coffee, the beds
15 walk	o a problem

Write your answers here.

1	2	3	4	5	6	7	8	9	10	11	12	13	14	15

Useful verbs 3

Complete the sentences below with a suitable verb. Use each verb once only. Choose from the following:

agree	earn	know	sell
borrow	explain	learn	start
call	forget	let	thank
cost	hear	live	travel
describe	help	prefer	wait

1 She tried to _____ why she was late.
2 I'd like to _____ everyone for helping me with the party.
3 'Do you like jazz?'
  'No, I _____ pop music.'
4 Is there anyone in the class who doesn't _____ what the word 'greedy' means?
5 'I think women are much better drivers than men are.'
  'Yes, I _____!'
6 'How much does this book _____, please?'
  '£8.99.'
7 'When did you _____ to drive?'
  'When I was seventeen.'
8 I'm going to _____ my house. Do you know anyone who wants to buy it?
9 Will you _____ me kiss you if I ask you to marry me?
10 'Can you _____ what the man looked like, sir?'
  'Well, officer, he was tall and well-built with fair hair and a moustache.'
11 My mother always gets very upset if I _____ to send her a card on her birthday.

12 I _____ in Wales now. But I was born in New
Zealand.

13 I won't be long. Can you _____ for me?

14 'How much does a teacher _____ in this country?'
'About £20,000 a year, I think.'

15 He asked us to _____ him move the piano.

16 We usually _____ by air when we visit our son in
Germany.

17 We have decided to _____ our daughter Amanda,
after her grandmother.

18 Could you speak louder, please? We can't _____ at
the back.

19 'What time does the film _____?'
'At 7.30.'

20 If you need money, you can always try to _____
some from the bank.

Useful verbs 4

Complete the sentences below with a suitable verb. Use each verb once only. Choose from the following:

find	move	remember	take
hate	need	sign	talk
keep	promise	smell	think
lose	put	stay	understand
meet	recognize	study	want

1 'Do you _____ John's address?'
  'Yes, it's 27 Wood Lane.'

2 'How long are you going to _____ in Paris?'
  'About ten days altogether.'

3 She told me to _____ the milk and eggs in the
  fridge.

4 'Do you _____ it will rain tomorrow?'
  'Oh, I hope not.'

5 Could you _____ more slowly, please? Mario
  doesn't speak English very well.

6 'Do you like football?'
  'No, I _____ it!'

7 He had a thick, black beard so we didn't _____ him
  at first.

8 'Where did you _____ your husband?'
  'On a number 17 bus.'

9 She gave me a pen and asked me to _____ my
  name.

10 I've lost my lighter. Can you help me to _____ it?

11 'What do you _____ to be when you grow up?'
  'Alive and very rich.'

12 She asked me to _____ her books back to the library.

13 'Will you _____ to phone me as soon as you arrive?' 'Yes, of course I will.'

14 We're going to leave London and _____ to North Wales when we're 65.

15 I don't *speak* French very well, but I _____ quite a lot.

16 'Can you _____ something burning?' 'Oh dear! I forgot to switch off the oven!'

17 He gave the taxi-driver £10 and told him to _____ the change.

18 If you _____ hard, you should pass all your exams in the summer.

19 You _____ to be very strong and fit to be a ballet dancer.

20 I don't like playing tennis because I always _____. Even my grandmother beats me!

Prepositions of place 1

Look at the drawings below and write the missing prepositions in the sentences. Choose from the following:

above	at the corner of	down
across	at the end of	from
against	behind	in
along	below	in front of
at	between	on

1 He was waiting for us _____ the station.

2 The restaurant is _____ the bank and the supermarket.

3 He is standing _____ the mirror.

4 The Chinese restaurant is _____ Grove Road and Kelvin Road.

5 He lives in a flat _____ a greengrocer's.

6 She is walking _____ the stairs.

7 There are lots of flowers _____ the vase.

8 They are walking _____ the sea front.

9 The cat is sleeping _____ the bed.

10 The girl guide is helping the old man _____ the road.

11 There is a pub _____ the street.

12 The painting is _____ the clock.

13 He is leaning _____ a lamp-post.

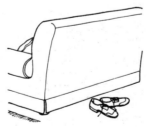

14 There is a pair of shoes _____ the sofa.

15 The village is only two miles _____ the sea.

113

Prepositions of place 2

Look at the drawings below and write the missing prepositions in the sentences. Choose from the following:

inside	opposite	through
into	out of	to
near	outside	towards
next to	over	under
on top of	round	up

1 The girl is jumping _____ the stream.

2 He is walking _____ the bus-stop.

3 There is a statue _____ the Town Hall.

4 The rain is coming in _____ a hole in the roof.

5 The money is _____ the safe.

6 The dog is asleep _____ the table.

7 She is getting
_____ bed.

8 The photograph
is _____
the bookcase.

9 He is pushing
his bicycle
_____ the
hill.

10 The bank is
_____ the
shoe shop.

11 The taxi
stopped
_____ the
cinema.

12 She lives
_____ the
park.

13 He is getting
_____ the
car.

14 A motorbike is
coming
_____ the
corner.

15 She is tying her
dog _____
a post.

Prepositions of time

Write the missing prepositions in the sentences below. You can use each preposition more than once. Choose from the following:

at	in	since
for	on	until

1 I usually get up _____ 7.30.
2 My wife and I haven't smoked _____ at least ten years.
3 Beethoven was born _____ the eighteenth century.
4 Many people in Britain put the cat out _____ night.
5 Bye, John. See you _____ Friday.
6 We haven't heard from James _____ last May.
7 My sister usually goes swimming _____ the weekend.
8 He always has a big party _____ New Year's Eve.
9 Pop music was really great _____ the 1960s.
10 I haven't seen Amanda _____ a long time.
11 We usually go shopping _____ Saturday mornings.
12 My father hasn't been to a football match _____ 1974.
13 Sarah and Paul got married _____ 1983.
14 Stay here _____ I come back.
15 Robert learnt to play the guitar _____ the age of twelve.
16 Her birthday is _____ June.
17 He always visits his parents _____ Christmas.
18 Do you have snow in your country _____ the winter?
19 I have been ill _____ nearly two weeks.
20 She will be fifty _____ 10th December. I hope she has a party.
21 We worked from nine o'clock _____ ten thirty.

Prepositions with nouns

Write the missing prepositions in the sentences below. You can use some of the prepositions more than once. Choose from the following:

at	for	on
by	in	with

1 He met his wife _____ a party.
2 There's a good film _____ television tonight.
3 Would you like to go out _____ a drink tonight?
4 What shall we have _____ dinner?
5 This music is _____ John Lennon.
6 'Where's Peter?'
  'He's _____ holiday.'
7 David hasn't got up yet. He's still _____ bed.
8 We always travel to France _____ air.
9 Help! Help! My house is _____ fire!
10 Would you like a cake or a biscuit _____ your coffee?

Prepositions with adjectives

Write the missing prepositions in the sentences below. You can use
some of the prepositions more than once. Choose from the following:

about	from	of
at	in	to
for		

1 My sister is very good _____ tennis.
2 Helen is afraid _____ dogs.
3 Sally is very interested _____ cars – especially sports cars.
4 Pamela has been married _____ Mark for fifteen years.
5 I'm tired _____ learning German. It's too difficult.
6 Do you know what Switzerland is famous _____?
7 She is very proud _____ being Scottish.
8 Don't ask me to join the choir. I'm really bad _____ singing.
9 His latest single is very different _____ his first one. It's
   hard to believe it's the same singer.
10 I'm sorry _____ the noise yesterday. It was my sister's
   birthday.
11 It was very kind _____ you to help us.
12 She told them she was sorry _____ not being at the meeting.
   But her son was ill.

Prepositions with verbs

Write the missing prepositions in the sentences below. You can use
some of the prepositions more than once. Choose from the following:

after	from	to
at	in	with
for		

1 She lives _____ London Road, near the post office.
2 Shall we go _____ the cinema tonight?
3 He tried to borrow £25 _____ his boss.
4 Yes, you're right. I agree _____ you.
5 Could you look _____ the children for me tonight? I have to
   go to a meeting.
6 They arrived _____ Manchester at 10.30.
7 Good morning. Could I speak _____ Ms Cummings, please?
8 I've lost my cat. Will you help me to look _____ her?
9 The teacher asked the pupils to look _____ the exercise on
   page 15.
10 I often listen _____ the radio when I'm driving.
11 She thanked us _____ helping her.
12 He is 35, but he still lives _____ his parents.
13 Let me introduce you _____ David Blake.
14 She asked the shopkeeper _____ a packet of cigarettes.
15 Do you believe _____ God?
16 I won't be long. Can you wait _____ me, please?

Useful phrases

Match the phrases or situations 1–10 with the correct responses a–j.

1 Excuse me, could you tell me the way to the library, please?

2 (*Someone is in danger. You want to warn him / her.*)

3 Do you need any help?

4 (*In a shop*) Anything else?

5 Have you got the right time, please?

6 It looks like rain.

7 I love Indian food.

8 (*You are on a bus. It is full. An old person gets on.*)

9 I don't like opera very much.

10 You're from Sweden, aren't you?

a Oh, I hope not.

b Neither do I.

c Sorry, I'm a stranger here too.

d Yes, that's right.

e Look out!

f So do I.

g It's all right, thanks. I can manage.

h Yes, it's two thirty.

i No, that's all, thank you.

j Would you like a seat?

Write your answers here.

1	2	3	4	5	6	7	8	9	10

Check 2

This is a check to see how many words you can remember from Section Four, Section Five and Section Six. Try to do it without looking back at the previous pages.

1 Which of the following is usually found in the kitchen?
   (a) a calf   (b) a meadow   (c) a grater   (d) a breeze
2 I usually _____ my own bread.
   (a) mash   (b) grill   (c) roast   (d) bake
3 What's this?

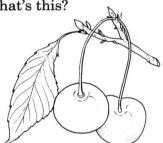

   (a) a strawberry
   (b) a grapefruit
   (c) a plum
   (d) a cherry

4 Which of the following is not a vegetable?
   (a) asparagus   (b) rhubarb   (c) beetroot   (d) leek
5 She bought a _____ of meat.
   (a) joint   (b) loaf   (c) carton   (d) bar
6 *(At a restaurant)* For a starter I'd like _____.
   (a) boiled potatoes   (b) fillet of plaice   (c) cheesecake
   (d) pâté with toast

7 What's the weather like?

    (a) It's foggy.

    (b) It's raining.

    (c) It's clearing up.

    (d) It's stormy.

8 Which of the following is usually a farm animal?

  (a) a bull   (b) a tortoise (c) a shark (d) a squirrel

9 Which of the following is not usually kept as a pet?

  (a) a rabbit   (b) a fox (c) a puppy (d) a hamster

10 Which of the following is an insect?

  (a) a frog   (b) a ladybird (c) a snake (d) a pigeon

11 What sound does a horse make?

  (a) It barks.   (b) It roars. (c) It neighs.   (d) It bleats.

12 What's this?

    (a) an avalanche

    (b) a hurricane

    (c) an earthquake

    (d) a volcanic eruption

13 There are twenty words hidden in the following word square. They are all groceries. See how many you can find. You can read vertically (*seven words*), horizontally (*seven words*) or diagonally (*six words*).

```
A K F T H E R C R R F G O S T P
R B A C O N O D M I N K M T E T
D E G O S B L M E A C B R E A D
C R O K A T L P R S D E I L B G
R O V E V P S C F A B M E O A S
E S R O G B I S C U I T S T G T
S H I N A V K E S S D R G R S I
O E L B F A U I O A F Q M Y E S
K B G E C L G R E G C B R E A B
H E W G F I A D N E J A N S A U
L E A V S I D K I S T S K E S T
P R E T U G J H E S W E A E S T
F R C H I P S N K S B C O T S E
I L F S A R C L B I M I L K D R
S O U P C H Q M I S L F A P I M
H G R E E C R I S P S E W I S S
```

14 In each of the following groups of four words, one does not fit in. Underline the word and try to say why it is different from the rest.

   (a) stream, lake, waterfall, meadow
   (b) cling-film, apron, kettle, rolling pin
   (c) avocado, melon, cabbage, pineapple
   (d) peas, carrot, green pepper, lettuce
   (e) cloudy, showers, drizzle, pouring

15 Complete the following sentences. To help you, the first letter of the answer is given.

   (a) The opposite of **sharp** is b_____.
   (b) The opposite of **easy** is d_____.
   (c) The opposite of **clean** is d_____.
   (d) The opposite of **wide** is n_____.

(e) The opposite of **tall** is s_____.

(f) The opposite of **rough** is s_____.

(g) The opposite of **hard** is s_____.

(h) The opposite of **strong** is w_____.

(i) The opposite of **full** is e_____.

(j) The opposite of **beautiful** is u_____.

16 Look at the drawing below, then tick (✓) any sentences that are correct.

(a) The armchair is opposite the sofa.

(b) The magazine is under the coffee table.

(c) The budgie is inside the cage.

(d) The stereo is on top of the bookcase.

(e) The plant is behind the armchair.

(f) The coffee table is between the sofa and the bookcase.

(g) The dog is sleeping in front of the fire.

124

(h) The cushion is on the sofa.

(i) The cat is asleep under the carpet.

(j) The armchair is next to the door.

(k) The clock is over the fireplace.

(l) The ashtray is behind the vase of flowers.

17 Read through the following sentences and try to work out what the missing words are. To help you, the first and last letters of the words are given.

(a) This plate is too hot to pick up. Pass me the o__n g___e, please.

(b) I'll have a b___h of grapes, please.

(c) You can buy a hammer and a screwdriver at the i_____r's.

(d) Tomorrow the weather will be dull and o_____t.

(e) A b_____d is a storm with heavy snow and high winds.

(f) The d_____t has lasted six months already. Let's hope we get some rain soon.

(g) A dog bit her when she was small. Since then she has been a____d of them.

(h) Could you e_____n what this word means?

(i) A knife is sharp and can be d_____s.

(j) We walked along the f_____h towards the village.

18 Say whether the following sentences are true (T) or false (F).

(a) A **brave** person is easily frightened.

(b) This car is not made in this country. It's a **foreign** car.

(c) Give me a drink, please. I'm very **hungry**.

(d) I'd like a **packet** of jam, please.

(e) He has never had an accident. He is always very **careful**.

(f) She went to the **off-licence** to buy a bottle of wine.

(g) He looked different, so I didn't **recognize** him at first.

(h) I'll see you **at** Sunday afternoon.

(i) You usually fry bacon in a **saucepan**.

(j) My two favourite vegetables are **Brussels sprout**s and **cucumber**.

125

19 Fill in the missing prepositions in the following sentences.

    (a) We usually get up _____ eight o'clock.

    (b) I haven't smoked _____ a long time.

    (c) _____ which century was Shakespeare born?

    (d) Her birthday is _____ 18th February.

    (e) She met her husband _____ a party.

    (f) What shall we have _____ breakfast?

    (g) He is very good _____ golf.

    (h) How long has Gareth been married _____ Samantha?

    (i) He lives _____ Kensington Road.

    (j) Thank you _____ helping me.

20 (a) Match the things on the left with the shop or building on the right. Draw lines between correct pairs.

bread, cakes	chemist's
cash a cheque	jeweller's
cigarettes, matches	tobacconist's
medicine, perfume	baker's
ring, watch	bank

    (b) Match the animal on the left with the sound it makes on the right. Draw lines between correct pairs.

a cat	quacks
a donkey	brays
a duck	howls
a pig	miaows, purrs
a wolf	grunts

(c) Match the verbs on the left with a suitable phrase on the right. Draw lines between correct pairs.

deliver	glasses
fail	an exam
ride	a bicycle
solve	a problem
switch off/on	the light
wear	letters

21 Complete the following dialogues (or situations).

(a)   (*You want to pay for a meal at a restaurant*)

    B: C_____

(b) A: Pam, this is Brian.

    B: H_____

(c) A: It looks like rain.

    B: Oh, I_____

(d)   (*You don't hear or understand something someone says to you*)

    B: S_____

(e) A: I can't come to the party. I've got to work.

    B: W_____

(f) A: Do you need any help?

    B: I_____

(g) A: Could you help me, please?

    B: Y_____

(h)   (*Someone has bought you a drink at the pub*)

    B: C_____

(i) A: You're Italian, aren't you?

    B: Y_____

(j)   (*Someone is looking very unhappy*)

    B: C_____

22 Look at the drawings and complete the crossword. Each of the missing words is a different verb.

Across →   **Down** ↓

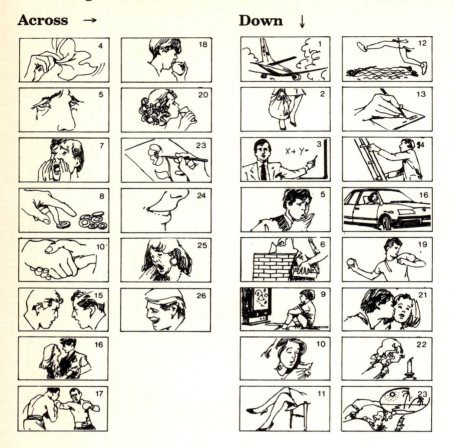

23 Here are thirty words in alphabetical order. Place each word under the correct heading. (Five words under each.)

ant	field	lemon	spider
bat	frying pan	mosquito	toaster
beetle	garlic	mountain	valley
blackberry	goat	octopus	wasp
bottle opener	grapes	onion	whale
bowl	hedgehog	peach	wood
cauliflower	hedges	pear	
celery	jug	radish	

Kitchen utensils   **Fruit**   **Vegetables**

_____   _____   _____

_____   _____   _____

_____   _____   _____

_____   _____   _____

_____   _____   _____

Animals   **Insects**   **In the countryside**

_____   _____   _____

_____   _____   _____

_____   _____   _____

_____   _____   _____

_____   _____   _____

Answers

Section One: People

Personal details (page 3)

1	Surname	4	Street	7	Nationality	9	Children
2	Christian name	5	Town/Village	8	Married or single	10	Job
3	Age	6	Country				

The family (pages 4 and 5)

1	children	7	son	13	nephew	19	grandfather
2	wife	8	parents	14	cousin	20	grandmother
3	daughter	9	grandchildren	15	mother	21	granddaughter
4	sister	10	grandson	16	father		
5	husband	11	uncle	17	niece		
6	brother	12	aunt	18	grandparents		

Parts of the body: The face (page 6)

4	cheek	5	eyebrow	1	jaw	7	nose
12	chin	9	eyelashes	13	lip	3	teeth
10	ear	11	forehead	15	mouth	8	throat
6	eye	2	hair	16	neck	14	tongue

Parts of the body: The body (page 7)

7	ankle	4	elbow	18	heel	5	thigh
19	arm	11	finger	13	knee	20	thumb
3	back	8	foot	9	leg	15	toe
14	bottom	12	hand	1	shoulder	17	waist
10	chest	2	head	16	stomach	6	wrist

Verbs to describe daily routines (pages 8 and 9)

1	wake up	9	have breakfast	17	start work	25	go to
2	goes off	10	eat	18	finish	26	phone
3	turn (it) off	11	listen to	19	have a break	27	find out
4	lie	12	leave home	20	have lunch	28	go to bed
5	get up	13	pop into	21	get home	29	fall asleep
6	have a shower	14	buy	22	have dinner	30	set
7	brush	15	catch	23	watch TV		
8	get dressed	16	read	24	meet		

Verbs you can use to talk about your life (pages 10, 11, and 12)

1 was born
2 started school
3 left school
4 went to university
5 started work
6 learnt to drive
7 met his future wife
8 fell in love
9 got engaged
10 got married
11 had children
12 bought a house
13 got a new job
14 moved
15 became a grandfather
16 got divorced
17 remarried
18 retired
19 lived by the seaside
20 died
21 was buried

Describing people: Clothes 1 (page 13)

8 boxer shorts
17 briefs/ underpants
4 jacket
11 jeans
14 jumper
9 pyjamas
20 raincoat/mac
5 shirt
15 shoes
2 slippers
1 socks
7 suit
19 swimming trunks
12 T-shirt
16 tie
10 tracksuit
18 trainers
3 umbrella
6 vest
13 waistcoat

Describing people: Clothes 2 (page 14)

4 belt
14 blouse
9 boots
17 bra
20 briefs/knickers
6 cardigan
11 coat
1 dress
16 dressing-gown
5 gloves
2 handbag
15 hat
8 nightdress
19 scarf
12 skirt
10 stockings
3 sweater
13 swimsuit
18 tights
7 trousers

Describing people: Physical appearance

1 (page 15)

age	height	hair	other words
about twenty-five, forty, etc.	about 165 cm	bald	has freckles
adult	of average height	blonde, fair	wears glasses
baby	short	curly	well-dressed
child	tall	dark	
elderly		grey	
in his twenties, fifties, etc.	**figure/build**	long, short	
middle-aged	fat	wavy	
old	has a good figure		
teenager	slim		
young	thin		
	well-built		

2 (page 17)

4 Paul
1 Emma
3 Pamela
8 Timothy
5 Mandy
6 Ken
7 Brian
2 Caroline

Describing people: Character

1 (page 18)

9	beautiful	7	happy	4	lazy	11	polite
3	generous	8	hard-working	10	mean	6	rude
1	handsome	2	intelligent	12	miserable	5	stupid

2 (page 19)

4	ambitious	5	impatient	3	selfish	6	sociable
7	boring	10	jealous	9	shy	1	tidy
2	imaginative	8	patient				

3 (page 20)

positive characteristics *(suggestion only)*

beautiful	polite
generous	ambitious
handsome	imaginative
happy	patient
hard-working	sociable
intelligent	tidy

negative characteristics *(suggestion only)*

lazy	boring
mean	impatient
miserable	jealous
rude	selfish
stupid	shy

Nationalities (pages 21 and 22)

1	English	6	American	11	Dutch	16	Chinese
2	Canadian	7	French	12	Australian	17	Brazilian
3	Italian	8	Scottish	13	Spanish	18	Greek
4	Saudi Arabian	9	Belgian	14	Japanese	19	Russian
5	Swiss	10	Turkish	15	Swedish	20	German

Useful phrases (page 23)

1 – d	4 – i	7 – c	9 – e
2 – j	5 – f	8 – h	10 – b
3 – g	6 – a		

Section Two: House and home

Places to live (pages 24 and 25)

4	block of flats	3	detached house
9	bungalow	5	flat
7	caravan	2	hotel
1	cottage	10	houseboat

8 semi-detached house
6 terraced house

Inside a house (page 26)

1	kitchen	5	front door	9	toilet	12	bedroom 1
2	living-room	6	staircase	10	landing	13	bathroom
3	dining-room	7	hall	11	spare room	14	balcony
4	study	8	bedroom 2				

Outside a house (page 28)

1	drive	6	hedge	11	roof	16	fruit trees
2	wall	7	pond	12	lawn	17	path
3	front garden	8	flower bed	13	chimney	18	fence
4	garage	9	back garden	14	patio	19	garden shed
5	gate	10	greenhouse	15	aerial	20	back door

Rooms of a house: The kitchen (page 30)

11	cooker/stove	18	forks	4	knives	3	sink
7	cupboard	6	freezer	1	oven	17	spoons
20	cups	12	fridge	10	plates	13	tap
15	dishwasher	16	frying pan	19	saucepan	2	tea towel
8	drawer	5	glasses	14	shelf	9	waste bin

Rooms of a house: The living-room (page 31)

4	armchair	5	curtains	2	lampshade	10	sofa
11	bookcase	13	cushion	12	mantelpiece	3	stereo
16	carpet	6	fire	9	painting	17	television/TV
14	ceiling	8	fireplace	1	plant	15	wallpaper
7	coffee table	18	lamp				

Rooms of a house: The bathroom (page 32)

10	bar of soap	7	electric razor	8	shampoo	2	toothbrush
6	bath	18	floor	1	shower	9	towel
15	bath mat	16	light switch	13	tiles	14	tube of
19	bathroom cabinet	12	mirror	4	toilet		toothpaste
11	comb	5	plug	20	toilet paper	3	wash-basin
		17	scales				

Rooms of a house: The bedroom (page 33)

8	alarm clock	18	brush	6	duvet	10	radiator
3	bed	1	chest of	17	hair dryer	4	rug
9	bedside table		drawers	15	mattress	11	sheet
14	bedspread	16	coat hanger	7	pillow	5	wardrobe
12	blanket	2	dressing-table	13	pillowcase		

Jobs and activities in the home (pages 34 and 35)

1	do the gardening	6	tidy up	9	clean the	12	do the ironing
2	do the polishing	7	do the hoovering		windows	13	do the washing
3	sweep the floor	8	do the	10	make the bed(s)	14	lay the table
4	bake a cake		washing-up	11	decorate	15	do the dusting
5	do the cooking						

Things in the home (page 36)

6	ashtray	2	electric iron	19	spanner	15	tray
16	bottle opener	11	hammer	8	tape measure	5	vacuum cleaner
12	bucket	7	key	18	tin opener	9	vase
1	cassette recorder	14	pair of scissors	4	toaster	17	video recorder/ VCR
13	corkscrew	20	radio	10	torch		
		3	screwdriver				

Useful phrases (page 38)

1 – g   4 – a   7 – b   9 – c
2 – f   5 – d   8 – i   10 – e
3 – h   6 – j

Section Three: Jobs, sport and leisure

Jobs 1 (page 39)

5	actor/actress	6	fireman	18	nurse	9	shop assistant
11	architect	20	lawyer	3	optician	4	traffic warden
16	bricklayer	2	librarian	7	policeman/	13	travel agent
1	butcher	14	lorry driver		policewoman	15	vet
17	dustman	10	mechanic	19	postman	8	waiter/waitress
12	estate agent						

Who does what? (page 42)

1	fireman	7	dustman	11	actor/actress	16	optician
2	lawyer	8	lorry driver	12	butcher	17	vet
3	nurse	9	policeman/	13	mechanic	18	estate agent
4	shop assistant		policewoman	14	traffic warden	19	librarian
5	travel agent	10	waiter/waitress	15	bricklayer	20	postman
6	architect						

Jobs 2 (page 43)

6	baker	5	cleaner	17	electrician	19	pilot
13	barber/	11	computer	7	farmer	12	plumber
	hairdresser		programmer	3	journalist/	4	secretary
18	businessman/	16	cook		reporter	8	soldier
	businesswoman	20	dentist	10	musician	14	surgeon
1	carpenter	2	doctor	15	photographer	9	teacher

Who uses what? (page 46)

1 – g	6 – q	11 – l	16 – d
2 – n	7 – t	12 – c	17 – o
3 – a	8 – b	13 – s	18 – j
4 – f	9 – h	14 – i	19 – p
5 – k	10 – r	15 – m	20 – e

Adjectives you can use to describe a job (page 47)

Free choice.

In an office (page 48)

6	blind	7	diary	12	hole punch	11	stapler
18	calculator	10	drawing pin	9	paper clip	4	telephone
1	calendar	13	fax machine	3	photocopier	14	typewriter
19	chair	16	file	15	printer	5	wastepaper
20	computer/PC	2	filing cabinet	8	rubber		basket
17	desk						

Places where you play or do sports (pages 50 and 51)

1	football pitch	3	golf course	5	tennis court	7	boxing ring
2	running track	4	ski slope	6	swimming pool	8	ice rink

Popular sports (page 52)

5	athletics	1	cycling	20	motor racing	10	squash
12	badminton	9	gymnastics	18	rugby	14	table tennis
19	basketball	11	hockey	2	sailing	7	weight-lifting
15	boxing	16	horse-racing	13	show-jumping	4	windsurfing
6	cricket	17	ice skating	3	snooker	8	wrestling

What do you use? (page 55)

f	athletics	k	cricket	d	horse racing	i	snooker
l	badminton, tennis	c	golf	h	ice skating	b	swimming
g	boxing	a	gymnastics	e	skiing	j	weight-lifting

Hobbies and pastimes (page 56)

5	aerobics	7	dressmaking	14	knitting	8	pottery
9	bird-watching	2	fishing	20	photography	15	reading
6	camping	11	gardening	12	playing cards	4	stamp collecting
10	cooking	13	going to evening classes	16	playing chess	19	watching TV
18	cycling			3	playing the piano		
1	dancing	17	jogging				

What are they called and where do you use them?

1 (page 58)

5	bicycle	11	magnifying glass	12	remote control	8	spade, wellingtons
7	binoculars	9	needles, wool	2	scissors, tape measure	4	tent
10	camera	6	recipe, frying pan				
3	fishing rod						
1	leotard						

2 (page 59) *Suggestions:*

1	aerobics, dancing	4	camping	8	gardening	11	stamp collecting
2	dressmaking	5	cycling	9	knitting	12	watching TV
3	fishing	6	cooking	10	photography		
		7	bird-watching				

Useful phrases (page 60)

1 – e	4 – c	7 – f	9 – b
2 – g	5 – h	8 – i	10 – d
3 – j	6 – a		

Check 1 (page 61)

1	(c)	nephew	4	(b)	vest	7	(d)	bungalow	9	(b)	dressing
2	(d)	cheek	5	(d)	tights	8	(a)	the			-table
3	(a)	ankle	6	(c)	mean			bathroom	10	(d)	vet

11 (page 62) (*Suggestion only. Other answers may be possible.*)

(a) son (*All the others are females.*)
(b) underpants (*All the others are worn by women.*)
(c) landing (*All the others are outdoors.*)
(d) dustman (*All the others wear a uniform.*)
(e) boxing (*All the others use balls.*)

12 (page 62)

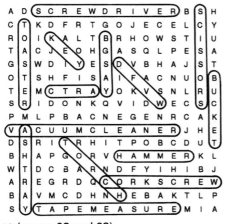

13 (pages 62 and 63)

(a) surname
(b) catch
(c) pyjamas
(d) sociable
(e) block of flats
(f) spare room
(g) fence
(h) cupboard
(i) hoovering
(j) traffic warden

14 (page 63) *Family tree:*

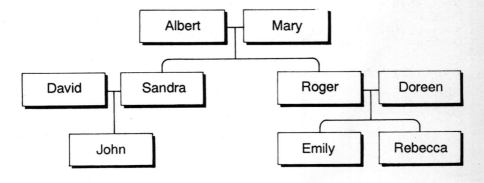

15 (page 64)

athletics – running track
bird-watching – binoculars
kitchen – fridge
cricket – bat
reporter – notebook

gymnastics – vault
bathroom – shower
tennis – racket
knitting – needles
plumber – spanner

16 (page 64)

(a) F (*You can't have a wife if you're a single man.*)
(b) T
(c) F (*You wear it under a blouse.*)
(d) F (*Impatient perhaps.*)
(e) F (*The washing. The washing-up is for plates, cups, etc.*)
(f) T

(g) F (*A leotard is worn by a dancer, a gymnast, etc.*)
(h) T
(i) F (*A cue is used in snooker. You hit the balls with it.*)
(j) T

17 (pages 64 and 65) *Correct order:*

She met her husband on holiday in July, 1964.   5
She started school at the age of five.   2
She got divorced in 1989.   9
She moved to Brighton when she was forty.   8
She left school in 1963.   3
She retired last year and now lives alone in a two-roomed flat.   10

Her first child was born in 1970.   7
She got married when she was twenty-one.   6
She was born in 1944.   1
She started work a month after she left school.   4

18 (page 65)

(a) tall, slim, young, long, dark, curly, jacket, tie, trousers, umbrella, imaginative

(b) elderly, seventy (*other suggestions possible*), short, grey, short, glasses, fat, cardigan, skirt, handbag, generous

19 (page 66) *Suggestions*:

(a) How do you do.
(b) Many happy returns!
(c) Congratulations!
(d) Thank you. The same to you.
(e) Yes, I'd love to.

(f) Say 'Cheese'!
(g) Stop, thief!
(h) Yes, please.
(i) Excuse me, please!
(j) Have a nice time!

20 (page 67)

In the kitchen	In the office	Parts of the face
saucepan	desk	cheek
oven	hole punch	chin
tap	filing cabinet	jaw
tea towel	paper clip	lip
waste bin	photocopier	nose

Parts of the body	Popular sports	Popular hobbies
waist	hockey	camping
knee	motor-racing	dressmaking
shoulder	show-jumping	photography
thumb	squash	pottery
wrist	wrestling	stamp collecting

21 (page 69)

Across
1 Dutch   3 American   4 Swiss   6 English   7 Belgian   10 Spanish   14 Saudi Arabian
15 Chinese   16 French
Down
2 Turkish   3 Australian   5 Swedish   7 Brazilian   8 Italian   9 Canadian   11 Scottish
12 Russian   13 Japanese

Section Four: Food, shops and shopping

Things we use in the kitchen (page 70)

6	apron	9	grater	3	microwave	10	scales
8	bottle opener	12	grill	13	oven glove	2	tin opener
4	bowl	5	jug	14	rolling pin	7	toaster
1	frying pan	11	kettle	15	saucepan		

Verbs to do with cooking (page 71)

1	grill	3	mash	5	fry	7	chop
2	roast	4	bake	6	grate	8	boil

How to make a good cup of tea (page 71)

Correct order:

1 Fill a kettle full of cold water. Let the
2 water come to the boil, but do not let it
3 go on boiling for very long. Pour
4 some of the water into a teapot to heat it
5 thoroughly. Pour the water away and
6 put in the tea, one teaspoon per person
7 and one for the pot. Take the teapot to
8 the kettle and pour the water on to the
9 tea while it is still boiling. Stir briskly,
10 put the lid on the teapot and let it brew
11 for several minutes. You will now have
12 a perfect cup of tea.

Fruit, nuts and berries (page 72)

5	apple	11	coconut	2	nuts	12	pineapple
10	avocado	18	grapefruit	1	orange	8	plum
17	banana	13	grapes	9	peach	15	rhubarb
14	blackberry	7	lemon	3	pear	4	strawberry
6	cherry	16	melon				

Vegetables (page 73)

7	asparagus	1	cauliflower	19	green/red peppers	16	onion
12	beans	8	celery			14	parsley
15	beetroot	5	corn on the cob	17	leek	11	peas
4	Brussels sprout	20	cucumber	9	lettuce	3	radish
18	cabbage	10	garlic	2	mushroom	6	tomato
13	carrot						

Groceries (page 74)

9	bacon	6	coke	21	milk	7	sausages
16	biscuits	23	cornflakes	8	mineral water	13	soup
20	bread	11	crisps	12	pie	19	spaghetti
10	butter	22	eggs	24	rice	3	sweets
5	cakes	1	fish	2	roast chicken	15	tea-bags
14	chips	17	meat	18	rolls	4	yoghurt

How we buy groceries (page 76)

1 – e	5 – l	9 – n	13 – g
2 – h	6 – a	10 – b	14 – j
3 – k	7 – i	11 – m	15 – c
4 – o	8 – f	12 – d	

Shops and shopping (pages 77 and 78)

1	card shop	7	barber's ...	13	toy shop	19	butcher's
2	furniture shop		hairdresser's	14	chemist's	20	shoe shop
3	newsagent's	8	post office	15	ironmonger's	21	launderette
4	tobacconist's	9	fishmonger's	16	record shop	22	café
5	baker's	10	bank	17	dry cleaner's	23	florist's
6	department store	11	greengrocer's	18	supermarket	24	jeweller's
		12	off-licence				

At a restaurant (page 79)

1–2	tomato soup, prawn cocktail	6–8	boiled potatoes, chips, runner beans
3–5	fillet of plaice, lamb chops, duck with orange sauce	9–10	apple pie and custard, fruit cocktail

Useful phrases (page 80)

1 – c	4 – h	7 – i	9 – b
2 – g	5 – a	8 – f	10 – d
3 – e	6 – j		

Section Five: The world of nature

Months and seasons (pages 81 and 82)

Suggestion only for Britain. Local variations possible.

Seasons	months	events
spring	March	Easter
	April	when young animals are born
	May	
summer	June	the longest day of the year
	July	when most people go on holiday
	August	when the school year ends
		when the weather is warmest
		Wimbledon tennis championships

autumn	September	bonfire night
	October	Hallowe'en
	November	Oscar prize-giving ceremony
		when the school year starts
winter	December	Christmas
	January	New Year's Eve
	February	Nobel day
		St. Valentine's Day
		the shortest day of the year
		when the weather is coldest

What's the weather like? (page 83)

1 It's raining.
2 It's very hot.
3 It's frosty.
4 It's below zero.
5 It's stormy.
6 It's foggy.
7 It's windy.
8 It's snowing.
9 It's cloudy.
10 It's sunny.
11 It's misty.
12 It's clearing up.

Weather forecast (page 85)

1 heavy snow
2 rain
3 fog and mist patches
4 dull and overcast
5 snow storms
6 showers and sunny periods
7 cloudy with sunny periods
8 high winds and showers
9 storms
10 dry and sunny

More words to do with the weather

1 (page 86)

a blizzard	a storm with heavy snow and high winds
a breeze	a light or gentle wind
a gale	a very strong wind
a shower	a short period of rain
changeable	changing from one type of weather to another
chilly	rather cold
drizzle	light rain falling in very small drops
overcast	dark with a lot of clouds in the sky
pouring	heavy rain
sunny spells	sun and clouds

2 (page 86)

1 a blizzard
2 overcast

Animals 1: Pets and farm animals (page 87)

9 bull
20 calf
14 cat
19 cock
10 cow
15 dog
6 donkey
13 duck
18 goat
12 goose
3 hamster
7 hen
11 horse
1 kitten
17 lamb
8 pig
2 puppy
5 rabbit
16 sheep
4 tortoise

Animals 2: Wild animals (page 88)

3 bat
8 bear
11 camel
18 dolphin
7 elephant
4 fox
16 giraffe
2 hedgehog
12 kangaroo
14 lion
10 monkey
6 mouse
20 penguin
1 rat
17 shark
5 squirrel
15 tiger
19 whale
9 wolf
13 zebra

Animals 3: Insects and other animals (page 89)

6	ant	4	fly	13	octopus	12	snake
10	bee	14	frog	11	pigeon	2	spider
3	beetle	1	ladybird	15	scorpion	7	wasp
9	butterfly	8	mosquito	17	snail	16	worm
18	crab	5	moth				

Animals sounds (page 90)

1 – e	5 – i	9 – d	13 – j
2 – g	6 – n	10 – m	14 – c
3 – l	7 – a	11 – b	15 – h
4 – o	8 – k	12 – f	

Natural disasters

1 (page 91)

1	hurricane	3	drought	5	forest fire	7	avalanche
2	flood	4	volcanic eruption	6	earthquake		

2 (page 92)

a	drought	c	volcanic eruption	d	hurricane	f	flood
b	earthquake			e	avalanche	g	forest fire

In the countryside (page 93)

1	waterfall	5	lane	9	meadow	13	lake
2	hills	6	footpath	10	valley	14	mountains
3	hedges	7	wood	11	main road	15	river
4	village	8	peaks	12	stream	16	field

Useful phrases (page 95)

1 – e	4 – h	7 – c	9 – g
2 – j	5 – a	8 – b	10 – d
3 – f	6 – i		

Section Six: Adjectives, verbs and prepositions

Adjectives: Common opposites (pages 96, 97 and 98)

1	ugly	7	dark	12	blunt	17	low
2	difficult	8	weak	13	smooth	18	small
3	narrow	9	old	14	closed/shut	19	empty
4	thin	10	dirty	15	new	20	soft
5	slow	11	unhappy/sad	16	dry	21	expensive/dear
6	short						

142

Useful adjectives 1 (page 99)

1	comfortable	5	alive	9	asleep	13	funny
2	foreign	6	bright	10	careful	14	cold
3	hot	7	famous	11	deep	15	busy
4	clever	8	free	12	brave		

Useful adjectives 2 (page 100)

1	late	5	hungry	9	important	13	straight
2	tired	6	married	10	modern	14	kind
3	rich	7	sweet	11	loud	15	thirsty
4	long	8	afraid	12	ill		

Adjectives to describe people and things (page 101)

1 – k	5 – l	9 – e	13 – h
2 – j	6 – c	10 – o	14 – d
3 – m	7 – i	11 – f	15 – n
4 – a	8 – b	12 – g	

Verbs that describe activities 1 (page 102)

11	bite	10	cry	20	kiss	12	smile
5	blow	13	draw	18	laugh	4	throw
7	build	2	dream	16	shout	15	watch TV
19	carry	14	drink	3	sit	9	wave
17	cough	1	drive	8	sleep	6	write

Verbs that describe activities 2 (page 104)

12	blow one's nose	10	die	6	paint	8	sneeze
7	climb	13	fight	5	pay	4	swim
14	count	15	fly	19	quarrel	20	teach
16	cycle	17	hold	3	run	1	wash one's hair
11	dance	2	jump	18	shake hands	9	yawn

Useful verbs 1 (page 106)

1 – d	5 – j	9 – a	13 – k
2 – l	6 – o	10 – i	14 – g
3 – n	7 – m	11 – f	15 – c
4 – h	8 – e	12 – b	

Useful verbs 2 (page 107)

1 – d	5 – l	9 – a	13 – b
2 – k	6 – c	10 – m	14 – h
3 – g	7 – i	11 – f	15 – e
4 – j	8 – n	12 – o	

Useful verbs 3 (pages 108 and 109)

1	explain	6	cost	11	forget	16	travel
2	thank	7	learn	12	live	17	call
3	prefer	8	sell	13	wait	18	hear
4	know	9	let	14	earn	19	start
5	agree	10	describe	15	help	20	borrow

Useful verbs 4 (pages 110 and 111)

1	remember	6	hate	11	want	16	smell
2	stay	7	recognize	12	take	17	keep
3	put	8	meet	13	promise	18	study
4	think	9	sign	14	move	19	need
5	talk	10	find	15	understand	20	lose

Prepositions of place 1 (pages 112 and 113)

1	at	5	above	9	on	13	against
2	between	6	down	10	across	14	behind
3	in front of	7	in	11	at the end of	15	from
4	at the corner of	8	along	12	below		

Prepositions of place 2 (pages 114 and 115)

1	over	5	inside	9	up	13	out of
2	towards	6	under	10	next to	14	round
3	opposite	7	into	11	outside	15	to
4	through	8	on top of	12	near		

Prepositions of time (page 116)

1	at	7	at	13	in	19	for
2	for	8	on	14	until	20	on
3	in	9	in	15	at	21	until
4	at	10	for	16	in		
5	on	11	on	17	at		
6	since	12	since	18	in		

Prepositions with nouns (page 117)

1	at	4	for	7	in	9	on
2	on	5	by	8	by	10	with
3	for	6	on				

Prepositions with adjectives (page 118)

1	at	4	to	7	of	10	about
2	of	5	of	8	at	11	of
3	in	6	for	9	from (or to)	12	for

Prepositions with verbs (page 119)

1	in	5	after	9	at	13	to
2	to	6	in	10	to	14	for
3	from	7	to	11	for	15	in
4	with	8	for	12	with	16	for

Useful phrases (page 120)

1 – c	4 – i	7 – f	9 – b
2 – e	5 – h	8 – j	10 – d
3 – g	6 – a		

Check 2 (pages 121 and 122)

1 (c) a grater
2 (d) bake
3 (d) cherry
4 (b) rhubarb
5 (a) joint

6 (d) pâté with toast
7 (c) It's clearing up.

8 (a) a bull
9 (b) a fox
10 (b) a ladybird

11 (c) It neighs.
12 (a) an avalanche

13 (page 123)

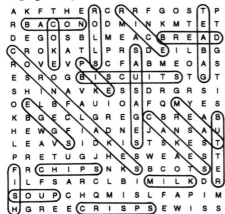

14 (page 123) *Suggestion only. Other answers may be possible:*

(a) meadow (*All the others are to do with water.*)
(b) apron (*It's the only one you can wear.*)
(c) cabbage (*It's a vegetable. All the others are fruit.*)
(d) carrot (*All the others are green.*)
(e) cloudy (*All the others are to do with rain.*)

15 (pages 123 and 124)

(a) blunt
(b) difficult
(c) dirty
(d) narrow
(e) short
(f) smooth
(g) soft
(h) weak
(i) empty
(j) ugly

16 (pages 124 and 125) *The following sentences are correct:*

(a), (b), (e), (g), (h), (k)

17 (page 125)

(a) oven glove
(b) bunch
(c) ironmonger
(d) overcast
(e) blizzard
(f) drought
(g) afraid
(h) explain
(i) dangerous
(j) footpath

18 (pages 125)

(a) F (*A brave person is not easily frightened.*)
(b) T
(c) F (*If you want a drink, you are thirsty.*)
(d) F (*A jar or a pot of jam.*)
(e) T
(f) T
(g) T
(h) F (*On Sunday afternoon.*)
(i) F (*You usually use a frying pan.*)
(j) T

19 (page 126)

(a) at
(b) for
(c) In
(d) on
(e) at
(f) for
(g) at
(h) to
(i) in
(j) for

20 (page 126)

(a)

bread, cakes	baker's
cash a cheque	bank
cigarettes, matches	tobacconist's
medicine, perfume	chemist's
ring, watch	jeweller's

(b)

a cat	miaows, purrs
a donkey	brays
a duck	quacks
a pig	grunts
a wolf	howls

(c) (page 127)

deliver	letters
fail	an exam
ride	a bicycle
solve	a problem
switch off/on	the light
wear	glasses

21 (page 127)

(a) Could I have the bill, please?
(b) Hello. Pleased to meet you.
(c) Oh, I hope not.
(d) Sorry?
(e) What a pity!
(f) It's all right, thanks. I can manage.
(g) Yes, certainly.
(h) Cheers!
(i) Yes, that's right.
(j) Cheer up!

22 (page 129)

Across

4 wave 5 cry 7 shout 8 count 10 shakehands (shake hands) 15 quarrel 16 dance
17 fight 18 bite 20 drink 23 draw 24 smile 25 yawn 26 laugh

Down

1 fly 2 carry 3 teach 5 cough 6 build 9 watchTV (*watch TV*) 10 sneeze 11 sit
12 jump 13 write 14 climb 16 drive 19 throw 21 kiss 22 blow 23 dream

23 (page 130)

Kitchen utensils	Fruit	Vegetables	Animals
bottle opener	blackberry	cauliflower	bat
bowl	grapes	celery	goat
frying pan	lemon	garlic	hedgehog
jug	peach	onion	octopus
toaster	pear	radish	whale

Insects	In the countryside
ant	field
beetle	hedges
mosquito	mountain
spider	valley
wasp	wood

146

Key words

The number after each word refers to the section in which the word appears.

about (*165 cm*) 1
about (*twenty-five, forty, etc.*) 1
above 6
across 6
actor 3
actress 3
adult 1
aerial (*noun*) 2
aerobics 3
afraid of 6
against 6
age 1
agree with (*someone*) 6
alarm clock 1; 2
alive 6
along 6
ambitious 1
American 1
ankle 1
answer (*verb*) 6
ant 5
apple 4
  apple pie and custard 4
April 5
apron 4
architect 3
arm 1
armchair 2
arrive at (*a place*) 6
ashtray 2
ask for (*something*) 6
asleep 6
asparagus 4
at 6
  at the corner of 6
  at the end of 6
athletics 3
August 5
aunt 1
Australian 1
autumn 5
avalanche 5
avocado 4

baby 1
back 1
  back door 2

back garden 2
bacon 4
bad at 6
badly paid 3
badminton 3
bake 4, 6
  bake a cake 2
baker (*job*) 3
baker's (*shop*) 4
balcony 2
bald 1
balls 3
banana 4
bank 4
bar of (*chocolate, soap*) 4
  bar of soap 2
barber (*job*) 3
barber's (*shop*) 4
bark (*a dog barks*) 5
basketball 3
bat (*animal*) 5
bat (*cricket*) 3
bath 2
  bath mat 2
bathroom 2
  bathroom cabinet 2
be: was born 1
  be: was buried 1
beans 4
bear 5
beautiful 1; 6
become: became a grandfather 1
bed 2
bedroom 2
bedside table 2
bedspread 2
bee 5
beetle 5
beetroot 4
behind 6
Belgian 1
believe in (*someone*) 6
below 6
  below zero 5
belt 1
between 6

bicycle 3
big 6
binoculars 3
bird-watching 3
biscuits 4
bite 6
bitter 6
blackberry 4
blackboard 3
blanket 2
bleat (*a sheep, a lamb bleats*) 5
blind (*noun*) 3
blizzard 5
block of flats 2
blonde 1
blouse 1
blow 6
  blow one's nose 6
blunt 6
boil 4
boiled potatoes 4
bookcase 2
boots 1
boring 1; 3
borrow (*something*) from (*someone*) 6
bottle of (*wine, mineral water, shampoo*) 4
bottle opener 2; 4
bottom 1
bowl 4
box of (*matches, chocolates*) 4
boxer shorts 1
boxing 3
  boxing ring 3
bra 1
brave 6
bray (*a donkey brays*) 5
Brazilian 1
bread 4
breeze 5
bricklayer 3
briefcase 3
briefs 1
bright 6

147

brother 1
brush (noun) 2
brush (verb) 1
Brussels sprouts 4
bucket 2
build (verb) 6
bull 5
bunch of (grapes, bananas, flowers) 4
bungalow 2
businessman 3
businesswoman 3
busy 6
butcher (job) 3
butcher's (shop) 4
butter 4
butterfly 5
buy 1
  buy: bought a house 1
buzz (a bee buzzes) 5
by 6

cabbage 4
café 4
cakes 4
calculator 3
calendar 3
calf 5
call 6
camel 5
camera 3
camping 3
can of (beer, coke) 4
Canadian 1
caravan 2
card shop 4
cardigan 1
careful 6
carpenter 3
carpet 2
carry 6
carton of (orange juice, yoghurt) 4
cash 6
cassette recorder 2
cat 5
catch 1
cauliflower 4
ceiling 2
celery 4
chair 3
changeable 5
cheap 6
cheek 1
cheesecake 4

chemist's 4
cherry 4
chest 1
chest of drawers 2
child 1
children 1
chilly 5
chimney 2
chin 1
Chinese 1
chips 4
chocolate gateau 4
chop 4
Christian name 1
clean (adjective) 3, 6
clean the windows 2
cleaner 3
clear up (It's clearing up.) 5
clever 6
climb 6
close (verb) 6
closed 6
cloudy 5
  cloudy with sunny periods 5
clubs 3
cluck (a hen clucks) 5
coat 1
coat hanger 2
cock 5
coconut 4
coffee table 2
coke 4
cold 6
comb (noun) 2; 3
comb (verb) 6
comfortable 6
computer 3
  computer programmer 3
cook (job) 3
cook (verb) 6
cooker 2
cooking (hobby) 3
corkscrew 2
corn on the cob 4
cornflakes 4
correct 6
cost (verb) 6
cottage 2
cough (verb) 6
count 6
country 1
cousin 1

cow 5
crab 5
creative 3
cricket 3
crisps 4
croak (a frog croaks) 5
cross 6
crow (a cock crows) 5
cruel 6
cry 6
cucumber 4
cue 3
cupboard 2
cups 2
curly 1
curtains 2
cushion 2
cut (verb) 6
cycle 6
cycling 3

dance 6
dancing 3
dangerous 3; 6
dark 1; 6
daughter 1
dead-end 3
dear 6
December 5
decorate 2
deep 6
deliver 6
dentist 3
department store 4
describe 6
desk 3
desserts 4
detached house 2
diary 3
die 6
  die: died 1
different from/to 6
difficult 6
dig 6
dining-room 2
dirty 3; 6
dishwasher 2
do the cooking 2
do the dusting 2
do the gardening 2
do the hoovering 2
do the ironing 2
do the polishing 2
do the washing 2
do the washing-up 2
doctor 3

dog 5
dolphin 5
donkey 5
down 6
dozen (*eggs*) 4
draw 6
drawer 2
drawing pin 3
dream (*verb*) 6
dress (*noun*) 1
dressing-gown 1
dressing-table 2
dressmaking 3
drill 3
drink (*verb*) 6
drive 2; 6
drizzle 5
drought 5
drunk 6
dry 6
  dry and sunny 5
dry cleaner's 4
duck 5
  duck with orange sauce
  4
dull and overcast 5
dustman 3
Dutch 1
duvet 2

ear 1
earn 6
earthquake 5
easy 6
eat 1
eggs 4
elbow 1
elderly 1
electric iron 2
electric razor 2
electrician 3
elephant 5
empty 6
English 1
estate agent 3
exciting 3
expensive 6
explain 6
eye 1
eyebrow 1
eyelashes 1

fail 6
fair 1
fall asleep 1
  fall: fell in love 1

famous 6
  famous for 6
farm 5
farmer 3
fast 6
fat 1; 6
father 1
fax machine 3
February 5
fence 2
field 5
fight 6
file 3
filing cabinet 3
fillet of plaice 4
find 6
  find out 1
finger 1
finish 1
fire 2
fireman 3
fireplace 2
fish 4
fishing (*sport*) 3
fishing rod 3
fishmonger's 4
flat (*adjective*) 6
flat (*noun*) 2
flood 5
floor 2
florist's 4
flower bed 2
fly (*noun*) 5
fly (*verb*) 6
fog and mist patches 5
foggy 5
foot 1
football pitch 3
footpath 5
for 6
forehead 1
foreign 6
forest fire 5
forget 6
forks 2
fox 5
free 6
freezer 2
French 1
fresh 6
fridge 2
frog 5
from 6
front door 2
front garden 2

frosty 5
fruit cocktail 4
fruit trees 2
fry 4
frying pan 2; 3; 4
full 6
funny 6
furniture shop 4

gale 5
garage 2
garden shed 2
gardening (*hobby*) 3
garlic 4
gate 2
generous 1
German 1
get dressed 1
get home 1
get up 1
get: got a new job 1
get: got divorced 1
get: got engaged 1
get: got married 1
giraffe 5
glasses 2
gloves 1; 3
go: went to university 1
  go off 1
  go to (*somewhere*) 6
  go to bed 1
  going to evening classes
  (*hobby*) 3
goat 5
goggles 3
golf course 3
good at 6
goose 5
grandchildren 1
granddaughter 1
grandfather 1
grandmother 1
grandparents 1
grandson 1
grapefruit 4
grapes 4
grate 4
grater 4
Greek 1
green peppers 4
greengrocer's 4
greenhouse 2
grey 1
grill (*noun*) 4
grill (*verb*) 4
grunt (*a pig grunts*) 5

gumshield 3
gun 3
gymnastics 3

hair 1
hair dryer 2
hairdresser (*job*) 3
hairdresser's (*shop*) 4
hall 2
hammer 2
hamster 5
hand 1
handbag 1
handsome 1
happy 1, 6
hard 6
hard-working 1
hat 1
hate 6
have a break 1
have a shower 1
have breakfast 1
have dinner 1
have lunch 1
have: had children 1
have: has a good figure 1
have: has freckles 1
head 1
hear 6
heavy snow 5
hedge 2
hedgehog 5
hedges 5
heel 1
height 1
help (*verb*) 6
hen 5
high 6
  high winds and showers
  5
hills 5
hiss (*a snake hisses*) 5
hockey 3
hold 6
hole punch 3
hollow 6
horse 5
horse-racing 3
hot 6
  hot: very hot 5
hotel 2
houseboat 2
howl (*a wolf howls*) 5
hungry 6
hurricane 5
husband 1

ice rink 3
ice skating 3
ill 6
imaginative 1
impatient 1
important 6
in 6
  in front of 6
  in his twenties, fifties,
  etc. 1
inside 6
intelligent 1
interested in 6
into 6
introduce (*someone*) to
  (*someone else*) 6
ironmonger's 4
Italian 1

jacket 1
jacket potatoes 4
January 5
Japanese 1
jar of (*jam, marmalade*) 4
jaw 1
jealous 1
jeans 1
jeweller's 4
job 1
jogging 3
join 6
joint of (*meat*) 4
journalist 3
jug 4
July 5
jump 6
jumper 1
June 5

kangaroo 5
keep 6
kettle 4
key 2
kilo of (*apples, potatoes,
  oranges*) 4
kind (*adjective*) 6
  kind of (*someone*) 6
kiss (*verb*) 6
kitchen 2
kitten 5
knee 1
knickers 1
knitting (*hobby*) 3
knives 2
knock 6
know 6

ladybird 5
lake 5
lamb 5
  lamb chops 4
lamp 2
lampshade 2
landing 2
large 6
late 6
laugh (*verb*) 6
launderette 4
lava 5
lawn 2
lawyer 3
lay the table 2
lazy 1
learn 6
  learn: learnt to drive 1
leave home 1
leave: left school 1
leek 4
leg 1
lemon 4
leotard 3
let 6
lettuce 4
librarian 3
lie 1
light (*adjective*) 6
light (*verb*) 6
light switch 2
lion 5
lip 1
listen to (*something*) 1; 6
litre of (*milk*) 4
live 6
  live: lived by the seaside
  1
  live in (*a place*) 6
  live with (*someone*) 6
living-room 2
loaf of (*bread*) 4
long 1; 6
look after (*someone*) 6
look at (*something*) 6
look for (*something*) 6
lorry driver 3
lose 6
loud 6
low 6

mac 1
magnifying glass 3
main course 4
main road 5
make 6

150

make the bed(s) 2
mantelpiece 2
March 5
married 1; 6
  married to 6
mash 4
mattress 2
May 5
meadow 5
mean (adjective) 1
meat 4
mechanic 3
meet 1; 6
  meet: met his future
  wife 1
melon 4
miaow (a cat miaows) 5
microwave 4
middle-aged 1
milk 4
mineral water 4
mirror 2
miserable 1
misty 5
modern 6
monkey 5
mosquito 5
moth 5
mother 1
motor racing 3
mountains 5
mouse 5
mouth 1
mouth mirror 3
move 6
  move: moved 1
mushroom 4
musical instrument 3
musician 3

narrow 6
nationality 1
near 6
neck 1
need 6
needles 3
neigh (a horse neighs) 5
nephew 1
new 6
newsagent's 4
next to 6
niece 1
nightdress 1
nose 1
notebook 3
November 5

nurse 3
nuts 4

October 5
octopus 5
of average height 1
off-licence 4
old 1; 6
on 6
  on fire 6
  on top of 6
onion 4
open (adjective) 6
opposite 6
optician 3
orange (noun) 4
out of 6
outside 6
oven 2; 3
oven glove 4
over 6
overcast 5

packet of (biscuits,
  cornflakes, cigarettes) 4
paint (verb) 6
painting 2
paper clip 3
parallel bars 3
parents 1
parsley 4
pâté with toast 4
path 2
patient (adjective) 1
patio 2
pay 6
PC (computer) 3
peach 4
peaks 5
pear 4
peas 4
penguin 5
personal details 1
phone (verb) 1
photocopier 3
photographer 3
photography 3
pie 4
pig 5
pigeon 5
pillow 2
pillowcase 2
pilot 3
pineapple 4
pint of (milk) 4
pipes 3

plane 3
plant (noun) 2
plates 2
play 6
playing cards (hobby) 3
playing chess (hobby) 3
playing the piano (hobby)
  3
plug 2
plum 4
plumber 3
policeman 3
policewoman 3
polite 1
pond 2
poor 6
pop into 1
post 6
postman 3
post office 4
pot of (jam, marmalade) 4
pottery 3
pound of (apples, potatoes,
  oranges) 4
pour (It's pouring.) 5
prawn cocktail 4
prefer 6
printer 3
promise 6
proud of 6
puppy 5
purr (a cat purrs) 5
put 6
pyjamas 1

quack (a duck quacks) 5
quarrel (verb) 6

rabbit 5
racket 3
radiator 2
radio 2
radish 4
rain (It's raining.) 5
rain (noun) 5
raincoat 1
rat 5
read 1
reading (hobby) 3
recipe 3
recognize 6
record shop 4
red peppers 4
remarry: remarried 1
remember 6
remote control (for TV) 3

reporter 3
retire: retired 1
rhubarb 4
rice 4
rich 6
ride 6
river 5
roar (*a lion roars*) 5
roast (*verb*) 4
roast beef 4
roast chicken 4
roast lamb with mint
    sauce 4
rolling pin 4
rolls (*noun*) 4
roof 2
rough 6
round 6
rubber 3
rude 1
rug 2
rugby 3
run 6
runner beans 4
running shoes 3
running track 3
Russian 1

sad 6
saddle 3
sailing 3
salad 4
saucepan 2; 3; 4
Saudi Arabian 1
sausages 4
saw (*noun*) 3
scales 2; 4
scalpel 3
scarf 1
scissors (*pair of ...*) 2; 3
scorpion 5
Scottish 1
screwdriver 2; 3
secretary 3
selfish 1
sell 6
semi-detached house 2
September 5
set (*the alarm clock*) 1
shake hands 6
shampoo 2
shark 5
sharp 6
sheep 5
sheet 2
shelf 2

shirt 1
shoe shop 4
shoes 1
shop assistant 3
short 1; 6
shoulder 1
shout 6
show-jumping 3
shower (*noun*) 2
shower (*of rain*) 5
showers and sunny
    periods 5
shut (*adjective*) 6
shy 1
sign (*verb*) 6
since 6
sing 6
single 1
sink (*noun*) 2
sirloin steak 4
sister 1
sit 6
skates 3
ski slope 3
ski stick 3
skilled 3
skirt 1
sleep 6
slim 1
slippers 1
slow 6
small 6
smell (*verb*) 6
smile (*verb*) 6
smoke (*verb*) 6
smooth 6
snail 5
snake 5
sneeze (*verb*) 6
snooker 3
snow: (*It's snowing.*) 5
    snow storms 5
sociable 1
socks 1
sofa 2
soft 6
soldier 3
solve 6
son 1
sorry about 6
sorry for 6
soup 4
spade 3
spaghetti 4
Spanish 1

spanner 2; 3
spare room 2
speak 6
    speak to (*someone*) 6
spell (*verb*) 6
spend 6
spider 5
spoons 2
spring 5
squash 3
squeak (*a mouse squeaks*)
    5
squirrel 5
staircase 2
stamp collecting 3
stapler 3
start 6
    start: started school 1
    start: started work 1
starters 4
stay 6
stereo 2
stethoscope 3
sticky 6
stockings 1
stomach 1
storms 5
stormy 5
stove 2
straight 6
strawberry 4
    strawberry ice-cream 4
stream 5
street 1
stressful 3
study (*room*) 2
study (*verb*) 6
stupid
suit 1
summer 5
sunny 5
    sunny spells 5
supermarket 4
surgeon 3
surname 1
sweater 1
Swedish 1
sweep the floor 2
sweet (*adjective*) 6
sweets 4
swim 6
swimming pool 3
swimming trunks 1
swimsuit 1; 3
Swiss 1

switch *(it)* off 6
switch *(it)* on 6

T-shirt 1
table tennis 3
take 6
talk 6
tall 1; 6
tap 2
tape measure 2; 3
tea-bags 4
tea towel 2
teach 6
teacher 3
teenager 1
teeth 1
telephone 3
television 2
tell 6
tennis court 3
tent 3
terraced house 2
thank 6
 thank *(someone)* for
 (doing something) 6
thigh 1
thin 1; 6
think 6
thirsty 6
throat 1
through 6
throw 6
thumb 1
tidy *(adjective)* 1
tidy up 2
tie *(noun)* 1
tiger 5
tights 1
tiles 2
tin of *(soup, sardines, cat
 food)* 4
tin opener 2; 4
tired 6
 tired of 6
to 6
toaster 2; 4
tobacconist's 4
toe 1
toilet 2
 toilet paper 2
tomato 4
 tomato soup 4
tongue 1
toothbrush 2
toothpaste *(tube of …)* 2

torch 2
tortoise 5
towards 6
towel 2
town 1
toy shop 4
tracksuit 1
tractor 3
traffic warden 3
trainers 1
travel *(verb)* 6
travel agent 3
tray 2
trousers 1
true 6
tub of *(margarine)* 4
Turkish 1
turn *(it)* off 1
TV 2
typewriter 3

ugly 6
umbrella 1
uncle 1
under 6
underpants 1
understand 6
unhappy 6
unskilled 3
unsuitable for a man 3
unsuitable for a woman 3
until 6
up 6

vacuum cleaner 2, 3
valley 5
vase 2
vault 3
VCR 2
vegetables 4
vest 1
vet 3
video recorder 2
village 1; 5
volcanic eruption 5
volcano 5

waist 1
waistcoat 1
wait 6
 wait for *(someone)* 6
waiter 3
waitress 3
wake up 1
walk 6
wall 2

wallpaper 2
want 6
wardrobe 2
wash-basin 2
wash one's hair 6
wasp 5
waste bin 2
wastepaper basket 3
watch TV 1; 6
 watching TV *(hobby)* 3
waterfall 5
wave *(verb)* 6
wavy 1
weak 6
wear 6
 wear: wears glasses 1
weight-lifting 3
weights 3
well-built 1
well-dressed 1
well-paid 3
wellingtons 3
wet 6
whale 5
wide 6
wife 1
windsurfing 3
windy 5
winter 5
with *(your coffee)* 6
wolf 5
wood *(material)* 3
wood *(trees)* 5
wool 3
word processor 3
worm 5
wrestling 3
wrist 1
write 6

yawn *(verb)* 6
yoghurt 4
young 1, 6

zebra 5